Good Arguments

SECOND EDITION

Good Arguments

An Introduction to Critical Thinking

C. A. Missimer

Prentice Hall, Englewood Cliffs, New Jersey 07632

Library of Congress Cataloging-in-Publication Data

Missimer, C. A.
Good arguments : an introduction to critical thinking / C.A. Missimer. -- 2nd ed.
p. cm.
ISBN 0-13-360322-9
1. Logic. 2. Critical thinking. I. Title.
BC177.M57 1990
168--dc20 89-22936
CIP

Editorial/production supervision: Ann Mohan
Cover design: Jeanette Jacobs
Manufacturing buyer: M. Woerner

Printed in the United States of America
10 9 8 7 6 5 4 3 2 1

ISBN 0-13-360322-9

Prentice-Hall International (UK) Limited, *London*
Prentice-Hall of Australia Pty. Limited, *Sydney*
Prentice-Hall Canada Inc., *Toronto*
Prentice-Hall Hispanoamericana, S.A., *Mexico*
Prentice-Hall of India Private Limited, *New Delhi*
Prentice-Hall of Japan, Inc., *Tokyo*
Simon & Schuster Asia Pte. Ltd., *Singapore*
Editora Prentice-Hall do Brasil, Ltda., *Rio de Janeiro*

Still dedicated to everyone who loves to browse through books—
If that doesn't include you yet,
then I dedicate this book to you in advance.

I gratefully acknowledge the assistance of Steve Carlson; our conversations on the nature of evidence were clarifying and most enjoyable.

CONTENTS

PREFACE

It continually amazes me when, after telling people that I teach thinking skills, many gaze away sadly and sigh, "Gee, I'm not very logical." Their distressing conclusion is, I would argue, not warranted! If you are a person who believes that you are not very logical, you may be in for a surprise. My reason for claiming that you are quite logical is that you use perfect logic to make hundreds of decisions each day.

"But," you may logically reply, "those are usually easy decisions. I have a hard time following the reasoning in a number of books I've tried to read." In this book you will learn how to recognize the parts of thought (for instance, conclusion, reasons, assumptions) that you have used for most of your life. Once you understand these parts of thought, you will be able to recognize the structures of even the most complicated arguments, which share important features with your daily decisions.

You may want to think about two assumptions underlying this book. One is that your time is best spent on a dozen basic workhorses of reason, rather than on learning many aspects of reasoning. Time-management authority Alan Lakein argues that in many areas of life an "80/20 rule" exists: For 80% of our meals we use 20% of our recipes, 80% of the time we use 20% of our wardrobe, 80% of the TV we watch consists of our few favorite shows. Lakein, of course, doesn't mean that these are exact percentages. He's making the point that most of the time we rely on a few basics. I have proceeded on the assumption that the same is true of thinking skills. There are many more than twelve concepts in informal logic, not to mention the rigors of formal logic. However, you will be best served by learning to manipulate the basic workhorses of reason, that 20%, as it were, frequently or always used in critical thinking.

The second assumption is that it is vital to practice the common phrases that indicate the structure of critical thinking. These phrases appear in boldface throughout the book.*

*This preface contains a few of the commonly used phrases that this book will show you how to argue with:

I would argue that
My reason is
[a claim is] not warranted
On the assumption that

My hope is that you will become at ease in recognizing the structure of critical thinking and begin a lifetime of fascination, reading others' good arguments and creating your own across a wide spectrum of subjects. Have fun!

C. Missimer
Seattle, Washington

Good Arguments

CHAPTER ONE

WELCOME TO THE COMMUNITY OF THINKERS

ACTUALLY, YOU'RE ALREADY A MEMBER

The fact that you were able to grasp what the preface was about indicates that you already possess critical thinking skills. In fact, you're far more skilled at critical thinking than you know. This book will help you to realize what you already know, and help you to build on it. And just as you've been a skilled thinker most of your life without necessarily being conscious of it, you have been a contributor to the community of thinkers too. Members of this community address one another largely through the use of arguments, whether in conversations, articles, or books.

THE DOZEN BASICS

To argue is to try to convince someone else that your point of view is right. Everyone reading this book has made scores of arguments. Good arguments are structured with these twelve features:

1. definition and distinction
2. issue

3. conclusion
4. reasons
5. alternative arguments
6. evidence
7. truth
8. consistency
9. warranted inference
10. assumptions
11. implications
12. prescription

These are concepts which a critical thinker must be able to use in order to appraise arguments. You will be handling all of these features in their appropriate language with ease by the end of the book. They are the basic stuff of critical thinking. All arguments display most, if not all, of these features.

If these features are unfamiliar, you may doubt that you will be able to use a number of foreign concepts within a few weeks, all of them at the same time. You have, however, already learned to perform any number of involved tasks, much as a cyclist downshifts and makes a left turn at a busy intersection while watching out for cars and people. Almost everything that is difficult initially becomes easy with habit.

First, I want to make you aware of how often you use the notions of definition, distinction, and argument. You will find about 20 phrases in boldface in this chapter which show different ways that critical thinkers express these concepts. Try to get used to these phrases, start using them in everyday discussions, and be on the lookout for them. These phrases are the "noises" that critical thinkers make.

DEFINITIONS

How many times in your life have you said "What do you mean?" Or, perhaps, in informal talk, "Whaddyamean?"

> LINDA: I thought that was a terrible game. Bah! 68–0.
> SALLY: Whaddyamean, "terrible"? The score may have been 68–0, but the winning team made so many superb plays!

The same principle of "whaddyamean" applies in critical thinking. When you write, you should say "Whaddyamean" to yourself a lot. You define or explain the meaning of your main terms that might be misunderstood. Those last four words are important—you'd almost never need to define "oak tree" or "elephant." If you had to define every word you used, you'd end up defining your definitions and never even get around to making your point. By now you may be muttering, "Well, dang it, how much defining should I do and expect others to do?" As a rule of thumb a writer should think about defining roughly one or two terms in a five-hundred-word essay. Abstract terms—the words for things you can't see, touch, or taste, such as "terrible," "justice," "natural," even "argument"—are more elastic and usually need defining.

So, *define what could be misunderstood, especially the abstract.* Here are some examples:

> **By the term** "community" in the chapter title, **I mean** participation in common.
> "Community" **means** participation in common.
> He used "community" **in the sense of** participation of people in a common activity.

Note the quotation marks around the term to be defined. Always use them. The quotation marks are important, emphasizing to the reader that the writer is setting up the ground rules to talk about "this important word."

You can get definitions from the dictionary. But one word about them. Because abstract terms such as "community" are harder to pin down, they are liable to have several dictionary definitions. Choose the one(s) you mean carefully.

Distinctions

In *defining* a term you say for sure what's *inside* the limits of your term. When you draw a *distinction* between your term and another, you say what's *outside* the limits of your term. Together, definition and distinction are a pair of pincers that grab hold of a slippery term. For instance, here are a definition and a distinction, both taken from a dictionary:

> By "argue" in this book I mean "maintain" or "assert"; I would distinguish this sense of argue from "quarrel" or "bicker."

With a definition you show what you mean (*within* your term: here, maintain, assert); with a distinction you show what you *don't* mean (*outside* your term: here, quarrel, bicker).

> The author **makes a distinction between** "community" in the sense of participating in a common activity *and* "community" in the sense of living in the same district or city.
>
> She **drew a distinction between** being easygoing **and** being lazy.

In the baseball example above, Sally drew a distinction between Linda's definition of "terrible" (68–0) and hers (no superb plays). In everyday talk, people often make distinctions by responding, "But that's not the same thing!" Can you think of any instances in which you'd use that phrase to draw a distinction?

To sum up: In any discussion, *show what you mean and what you don't mean by your major ideas, particularly the abstract ones; expect others to do likewise.*

False Dichotomy: Distinction Run Amok

Someone who creates a distinction that doesn't in fact exist can be said to have created "a false dichotomy." For instance, if I claim that either you're a serious student or you love to party, I hope I have created a false dichotomy: You can be both academically ambitious and party-loving; you just can't fulfill both sides of your nature at the same time.

Other examples:

> He argued that the slogan People, Not Profits **creates a false dichotomy between** making money **and** making people happy.
>
> In her speeches, she **raised a false distinction between** totalitarian **and** authoritarian regimes.
>
> The reader mistakenly thought that if ideas were expressed simply and enjoyably, they were not important. He **thereby created a false dichotomy between** the simple **and** the significant.

The following is an amusing claim of a false distinction:

> If you bet on a horse, that's gambling. If you bet you can make three spades, that's entertainment. If you bet cotton will go up three points [in the commodities market] that's business. See the difference?[1]

Chiding for Failing to Make Distinctions

People can argue about whether a distinction is a valid one or is a false dichotomy. It can also be argued that a person has failed to make a distinction:

> While arguing that most people are selfish most of the time, the author **failed to make a distinction between** self-regarding acts, such as sleeping, **and** acts against others, such as stealing.
>
> In claiming that everyone over sixty-five should receive social security payments, the proponents of the bill **are confusing two groups:**

those who really need these benefits and those who merely qualify for them but don't need them.

The key is to seek out and reflect on definition and distinction whenever an argument presents them.

ARGUMENT

In this book, we'll never mean "argument" in the sense of a quarrel; however, we will be using "argument" in two senses because it often occurs in both ways. To keep them distinct,* I have called one the *loose* sense of argument and the other the *strict* sense of argument. Remember the phrases "in the loose sense" and "in the strict sense"—they'll come in handy when you make distinctions.

The Loose Sense

The loose sense of "argue" is the way it was defined above, to maintain or assert. Here are some examples showing how to use "argue" in this way:

> **He argued that** it is better to know some of the questions than all of the answers.[2]
>
> Lily Tomlin **made the argument that** reality is a crutch for people who can't cope with drugs.[3]
>
> **I would argue** with Goethe **that** the intelligent person finds almost everything ridiculous, the sensible person hardly anything.[4] (This phrase means "I am actually arguing that" or "I would *agree* with Goethe"; if you mean to disagree you'd say, "I would take issue with Goethe" or "I would argue against Goethe's position that. . . .")

Maybe . . . and maybe not The term "argument" occurs frequently in this loose sense of making a claim about what is true. The word is wonderful in that it helps put the hearer in balance. While indicating that an assertion is clearly being brought forward, "argue" acknowledges that the assertion is just that—a *claim* that something is true. In fact, almost everything *is* a claim—or so I'm claiming!

*See how useful distinctions are? "Argument" has been distinguished in three important ways.

The words "argument," "assertion," and "claim" help you to maintain that critical balance between accepting and rejecting an idea so that you can look it over at leisure. In short, use of the terms "argue" and "claim" helps you to think "Maybe that's true, but maybe not."

Advice For the sake of developing your critical skills, and for the fun of it, try thinking of everything you hear and read as an argument, a claim, an idea to which you can respond "maybe; maybe not," rather than accept it as a given fact. It's impossible to actually think of *every* claim in that way, because of our overwhelming tendency to accept what we're told, but take this as a challenge (a "maybe not").* In the course of this book you will soon learn to sort out the likelihood of various types of claims (see chapters 4 and 12).

Your next move It's the addition of reasons that gives an argument needed backing. So when someone makes an argument or claim in the loose sense, your next move is to ask for reasons to support or back up the claim. Some ways of making that move:

> "**What are your reasons** for making that argument?"
> "**Why do you make that assertion?**"

Or, when analyzing a piece of writing in which the author made a claim but didn't give reasons why the reader should agree:

> The author argued that reality was just a crutch for people who can't cope with drugs, **but gave no reasons** to support this claim.

The Strict Sense of "Argue"

In its strict sense, to argue is to claim that something should be thought or done and to give a reason why it should be thought or done. For example, following this discussion I'm going to make an argument. I'll claim that reasoning with people is the best way to persuade them and then explain why I think so. A formal argument has at least one claim with at least one reason to support or back up that claim. *It's the addition of reasons that distinguishes an argument in the strict sense from an argument in the loose sense.* Reasons are needed to give most claims substance.

An example of an argument of the strict sort You may have noticed that the common "noises of a critical thinker" in this book appear in

*Some exceptions are greetings, such as "hello," or questions, "Is that a gefilte fish sandwich?" However, we're all aware of "leading questions" that contain claims, such as the famous "When is the last time you beat your wife?" And what about "Ow!"—is that a claim?

boldface type. When you come to these phrases, repeat them, aloud if you can get away with it. Hearing information is a memory aid. Underlining is important too. Both come down to repetition, and the more you repeat, the easier it will be to remember these phrases. The following argument includes a number of crucial terms:

> Argument is by far the best way to get another person to believe or to do something. First, **let me define** the sense in which I mean "argument." **I mean it in the sense of** "reasoned persuasion to think or to act in a certain way." Others have **made the argument that** force or pure emotion are better ways to persuade, but I believe that those people are wrong, and I will in the course of the argument **make a distinction between** reason **and** these other techniques of persuasion.
>
> **My claim is this.** Reason is the best way to persuade anybody. **By** "reason" **I mean** "to explain why a thing should be done or accepted." When you reason with a person, you **by definition** respect both that person's mind and the idea you are presenting. You believe that your idea is compelling enough, is well-enough supported by good reasons for its truth, that another rational person, upon thinking about the idea, would accept it. You also permit that person to help you with your idea. The help can come in at least three forms. First, the person could come up with an even better idea based on your idea. Second, if your idea is flawed, the person could point out how that is the case and whether the idea can be salvaged by the support of better reasons. Third, by talking about the idea to other people you may be persuaded to abandon it in favor of a totally different, better idea.
>
> The major alternatives to argument are force and emotional blackmail. **Unlike*** argument, they respect neither the person's mind nor the idea enough to put these first. In fact, **I would argue that** force and pure emotion degrade both the idea and the mind of the person. (Incidentally, **I would accept the definition of** "pure emotion" **as** a type of force, but since it is rarely perceived in those terms, I'll deal with it separately.) People can be persuaded to act a certain way through force. For example, in a number of countries today, people who disagree with their governments are tortured or killed. Under that threat of death, the other people obey the dictates of their government. They don't obey because a reasoned and open discussion preceded some political consensus, but because they fear imprisonment or death. So the ideas that the government is promoting aren't trusted on their own merits, nor are the minds of the people.

*A handy term that points out a distinction.

There are milder examples of persuasion by force, for example, fear of job loss, but even these are very powerful. Finally, to take a blatant example of force, the individual who holds a gun to the cashier's head while robbing the liquor store is not making an argument that the gunman deserves the money!

The last alternative, pure emotion, can have almost as devastating effects as pure force. **I would distinguish** pure emotion **from** an argument that contains an emotional appeal. An emotional argument is still susceptible to reason. But just as with force, an individual exerting pure emotion over another wants that other to act or do a certain thing out of feeling. Thus, discussion is impossible, and failure to feel the same emotions is often seen as disloyalty. Emotional blackmail is often the result. "Emotional blackmail" **is here defined as** deliberately punishing a person for not agreeing by withdrawing emotionally. **In effect*** the blackmailer is saying, "If you don't agree with me I won't love you any more." Notice that in this case, as with force, the blackmailer does not appeal to the person's mind nor to the rightness of the idea itself. Sometimes emotional blackmail can exist over relatively small things, such as a friend threatening to cut off another friend for not agreeing (actually, if you're the friend, it's no small thing to you). In one of the worst instances of force by pure emotion in recent years, the Reverend Jim Jones convinced most of his nine hundred followers that to oppose him was to betray him and then led them to follow him in suicide as an act of loyalty. This kind of blind loyalty **must be carefully distinguished from** the loyalty to others we demonstrate by arguing with them when we think they are wrong.

In conclusion, reason by argument is the only means of persuasion that respects both the person one is persuading and the idea. Therefore, it is the best way to persuade.

Approach the argument You are either persuaded or not persuaded by this argument. In either case you should do some more thinking about it.

If you are persuaded by the argument (or by the point of view that is being argued), *what can you contribute* that would make the argument more persuasive? (As stated in the preface, that assumption is that arguments can always be made better, and it is assumed that you'll operate on that assumption too.) What does this argument need in the way of further definitions, distinctions, or factual claims? What else do you know that the author could have *added*? If you happen to think of a factual claim you

*A handy phrase for further defining.

heard in your history class, say, that the three greatest mass murders of this century were all committed by governments that didn't permit a loyal opposition, you can use that as contributory information in your critique of the previous argument.

Likewise, ask whether the author should *subtract* something, i.e., should *eliminate* some distinction or factual claim. Perhaps a term should not have been defined in a particular manner. You already know a lot that could be of critical assistance to the author, and even if you agree, think of ways you could enhance the argument by suggesting that the author remove something.

If you're not persuaded and you know why, you're on your way. But let's say that you just don't like the argument but don't know why. Take a few minutes to think about it.

Does it conflict with something you've experienced directly or learned about? For example, you might just have come from a psychology class in which you've learned about the power of the unconscious. You may be feeling uneasy because you're wondering how that information fits in with this argument that reasoning is the best way to persuade. Use that "lack of fit" between your psychology class and the foregoing argument. Raise the unconscious as posing a difficulty for the argument.

To take another instance, you may be the parent of a two-year-old, and that experience may well be giving you grave doubts about reasoning as the best method of persuasion. That conflicting experience can be raised to challenge the author to take it into account, perhaps with a further distinction.

See? You can't lose, no matter what you think of an argument, and neither can the arguer who is willing to benefit from your critique.

Putting your critique into words Here are some typical phrases to help you get started.

> **While I agree with Missimer's argument that** reason is the best method to persuade, **I think that the argument could have been stronger if** the author had:
>
> 1. **Defined** loyalty.
> 2. **Made a more careful distinction between** reason **and** force. After all, reason is a sort of force, isn't it? For instance, we speak of "the force of reason."
> 3. **Supported the argument. I disagree with Missimer's argument that** reason is the best method to persuade. The author **has not taken** the influence of the unconscious **into account.** Further, the author has **failed to distinguish between cases in which** adults have the time to reason with other adults, **and** those frequent

> instances when one person hasn't the luxury of reasoning with another, for instance when one has to deal quickly with people or when dealing with young children. Furthermore, Missimer has **created a false dichotomy between** reason **and** emotion.

Of course, you'd have to flesh out these comments with more examples, but you'd be well on your way to providing helpful criticism.

Agree to Disagree

Everyone has been stuck arguing in a circle with someone else: "Yes it is, not it *isn't, yes it is!*" It's clearly time to disengage. One way to back off would be, "Let's not discuss this any longer." That's better than getting into a fist fight, but it spells the death of communication on that subject. A better tack would be, "Let's agree to disagree until we get more information." Often people are disputing a fact, or a value judgment that hinges on a fact. Agreeing to disagree admits a sense of harmony and willingness on both sides to learn more and to resolve that dispute in the future.

SUMMARY

This chapter focused on three important concepts in critical thinking: definition, distinction, and argument.

1. The use and importance of "definition" and "distinction" were explicated: definition as an explanation of what is meant by a term; the importance of defining abstract terms; distinction as an explanation of some important difference within or between terms or ideas.
2. Two general uses to which critical thinkers put the term "argument" were discussed: argument in the loose sense of a "factual claim," a claim that something is true; argument in the strict sense of a "factual claim supported by a reason."

EXERCISES

1. Choose an appropriate critical thinking word or phrase from among those that appeared in **boldface type** throughout this chapter, and fill in the blanks. Try this example:

   James Thurber made an interesting remark. He ____________ that "you might as well fall flat on your face as lean over too far forward."

   If you put in "argued" or "claimed," good! "Said" and "thought" are out for the time being, because you're supposed to choose from among words or phrases which appeared in **boldface type** in this chapter.

   Try these:

   a. In the course of his ____________, he defined "endurance" as the quality of withstanding hardship or stress.

b. In his latest book, Byrne makes a careful ___________ between "natural" in the sense of occurring in nature and "natural" in the sense of normal.
c. In *The Open Society and Its Enemies*, Karl Popper ___________ that "argument rarely settles a question, although it is the only means for learning—not to see clearly, but to see more clearly than before."[5]

2. Are the following arguments in the strict sense or the loose sense?
   a. He claimed that laughter could help cure illness.
   b. The doctor argued that babies start laughing when they're about ten weeks old and by four years of age children laugh about once every four minutes.
   c. She argued that laughter is beneficial, her reason being that when you laugh hard you stimulate the alertness hormone catecholamine.
   d. Nurses argue that because they spend more time with patients, they see the effects of humor on patients better than physicians do.
3. Consider making an argument that sports are violent. What terms would you have to define? What distinctions could you foresee needing to make? Do any analogous activities come to mind which would help you to make your argument?

READING

1. Sir Karl Popper's notion of the "rational unity of mankind" points, as he asserts, to our indebtedness to others for all we can possibly know or understand. These "others" are members of the community of thinkers, of which we're also part. The following selection is taken from a longer argument by Popper that persuasion by reason is best. As you read it, notice how carefully he crafts his definition of "reason." Don't be intimidated by this passage. Think (as always) about what you might contribute to the argument.

The conflict between rationalism and irrationalism has become the most important intellectual, and even moral, issue of our time. Since the terms "reason" and "rationalism" are vague, it will be necessary to explain roughly the way in which they are used here. First, they are used in a wide sense; they are used to cover not only intellectual activity but also observation and experiment . . . Secondly, I use the word "rationalism" in order to indicate, roughly, an attitude that seeks to solve as many problems as possible by an appeal to reason, i.e. to clear thought and experience, rather than by an appeal to emotions and passions. This explanation, of course, is not very satisfactory, since all terms such as "reason" and "passion" are vague; we do not possess "reason" or "passions" in the sense in which we possess certain physical organs, for example, brains or a heart, or in the sense in which we possess certain "faculties," for example, the power of speaking, or of gnashing our teeth. In order therefore to be a little more precise, it may be better to explain rationalism in terms of practical attitudes or behavior. We could then say that rationalism is an attitude to listen to critical arguments and to learn from experience. It is fundamentally an attitude of admitting that *"I may be wrong and you may be right, and by an effort, we may get nearer to the truth."* It is an attitude which does not lightly give up hope that by such means as argument and careful observations, people may reach some kind of agreement on many problems of importance; and that, even where their demands and their interests clash, it is often possible to argue about the various demands and proposals, and to reach—perhaps by arbitration—a compromise which, because of its equity, is acceptable to most, if not to all. In short, the rationalist attitude, or, as I may perhaps label it, the "attitude of reasonableness," is very similar to the scientific attitude, to the belief that in the search for truth we need cooperation, and that, with the help of argument, we can in time attain something like objectivity . . . .

The fact that the rationalist attitude considers the argument rather than the person arguing is of far-reaching importance. It leads to the view that we must recognize everybody with whom we communicate as a potential source of argument and of reasonable information; it thus establishes what may be described as the "rational unity of mankind."[6]

Do you agree or disagree with Popper's argument? First reread "Putting Your Critique into Words," above. Then write a paragraph in which you use some of these phrases to assess his argument.

NOTES

[1]Blackie Sherrode, quoted in Andrew Tobias, *The Only Investment Guide You'll Ever Need* (New York: Bantam Books, 1983), p. 117.

[2]Adapted from Robert Byrne, ed., *The 637 Best Things Anybody Ever Said* (New York: Ballantine Books, a division of Random House, Inc., 1982), p. 23.

[3]*Ibid.*, p. 475.

[4]*Ibid.*, p. 63.

[5]Karl R. Popper, *The Open Society and Its Enemies* (Princeton, N.J.: Princeton University Press, 1971), II, p. 227.

[6]*Ibid.*, pp. 224–25.

CHAPTER TWO

THE BASICS
Issue, Conclusion, and Reason

REASONS IN STRICT ARGUMENTS

To reiterate an important point made in chapter 1, when critical thinkers hear a claim, the next move they make is to ask *why* they should believe that claim. For example:

> Claim: You should try to drive at or below 55 m.p.h.
> Critical thinker's question: Why?
> Reason offered: Statistics show that there are fewer fatalities when people drive at or below this speed.

That is an argument in the strict sense. The claim is supported by a reason. It's the bare bones of a strict argument, and it's just one point of view on the subject. The reason may not even be true. But still, it is an argument. Here is "argue" as it appears in both loose and strict cases:

> Loose case: Fritz argued that you should try to drive at or below 55 m.p.h.
> Strict case: Martina argued that you should try not to drive over 55 m.p.h., **because** statistics show that when people drive at or below that speed, fewer deaths occur.

The *issue* Fritz is arguing is whether you should drive at or below 55 m.p.h. Fritz *concluded* that you should not drive over 55 m.p.h. He gave no reason for his claim. Therefore it is a loose argument, a claim without a reason.

Loose arguments are perfectly acceptable and are made all the time (for instance, right now!). You need only recognize them as such so that you can go on to ask whether they require supportive reasons. Most of the time they do.

Martina argued that you should try not to drive over 55 m.p.h., because statistics show that when people drive at or below that speed, fewer deaths occur.

The *issue* she argued is whether you should try not to drive over 55 m.p.h. She argued for the *conclusion* that you should try not to drive over 55 m.p.h. The *reason* that she gave in support of her conclusion *is that* statistics show that when people drive at or below 55 m.p.h., fewer deaths occur. A reason, be it that of Martina or anyone else, is a claim presented to defend or to justify a belief in a conclusion.

If the notions of issue, conclusion, and reason are still fuzzy, the rest of this chapter is calculated to set you straight. If, on the other hand, you feel confident about these features, skip to the exercises at the end of the chapter and try your skill.

THE ISSUE

A crucial ingredient in paying close attention to an argument is trying to figure out exactly what is being claimed or talked about. "Exactly what he or she is claiming" is the issue. Other common words for "issue" are "question" and "subject." Following are some common phrases:

The author **deals with the issue of**

She **raised the question whether**

The **subject under discussion is whether**

When you care about some issue, it is extremely important to understand exactly what is meant, since you'll want to benefit from someone else's wisdom. Everyone does this automatically in life and death matters. If someone were to walk into the room where you are now sitting and say, "Smoke is filling up the building," you would probably respond with something like, "What? Is there a fire?" You instantly seek out the significant issue for you, namely, whether there is a fire and not just a hundred people smoking cigarettes, which may be the issue in the other person's mind. At the same time you are demanding to hear his conclusion ("Yes, there is a fire" or "No, there's no fire"). You thus make sure—before you run out of the building yelling—that you are not confusing your interpretation of the issue with the truth (at least as the intruder with the bad news sees it). Better that both of you should run out of the building yelling!

It is in less than life and death matters that we should cultivate this same spirited interest. One very handy way of locating the issue is to say to yourself, "The issue is *whether*," and then fill in the ending with what the author or speaker would say. In the previous example, the issue you raised was *whether* there is a fire. Sometimes an author will come right out and tell us, **"The issue** I'm dealing with is **whether** abortion is right or wrong."

In other cases an author can rightly assume that we'll figure out what the issue is about without being told outright. When the argument is short, the presumption is that we can easily see what it's about; when the argument is long, say in a book or article, the issue is usually part of the title. However, the author should come right out and say **"The issue is"** whenever the argument is long and the issue is *not* part of the title. I say "part of the title" because wherever the issue is found, in the title or in the body of the argument, it is most often *embedded* in the conclusion, whether written or spoken. You do not often find titles like *The Issue of Whether Abortion Is Right or Wrong*, but titles like *Abortion: Scourge of Society* or *Abortion—Every Woman's Right*. Both of these titles state conclusions, which happen to be opposed to one another.

Let's look at some further examples of conclusions; then I can show you an easy way to get at the issue when it's not stated outright.

THE CONCLUSION

The conclusion is the *decision* that the thinker has made about an issue. Unlike the issue, the conclusion of an argument is usually stated outright. It is often preceded by words just meant to let us know that this claim *is* the conclusion, the main point the person has been driving at. When, near the end of the argument, the author says, "In conclusion," or "In sum," or "Therefore," it is tantamount to saying, "This is that major idea that I, the author or speaker, want you to believe." A conclusion word is almost mandatory in a good argument if that argument is longer than a paragraph. The most popular word used to indicate a conclusion is "therefore." Other words that may show a conclusion are "in sum," and "so." Here is an example for each of them:

> The weatherman said on the news this morning that it's going to rain today. In fact, when I walked outside I noticed that it was clouding up. **Therefore,** *I'd better go back and get my umbrella.*
>
> The critical thinking instructor is notorious for giving tough quizzes. **So** *I should spend all day Saturday studying.*

> The roof leaks, the floors are warped, the drains are clogged, the foundation is full of termites. **In sum, this house needs a lot of work.**

To get at the exact *issue* for these brief arguments, all you need do is substitute the word "whether" for the conclusion words.

> *Issue 1:* **whether** I'd better go back and get my umbrella
> Conclusion: Yes, I'd better go back and get my umbrella.
>
> *Issue 2:* **whether** I'd better spend all day Saturday studying
> Conclusion: Yes, I'd better.
>
> *Issue 3:* **whether** this house needs a lot of work
> Conclusion: Yes.

You can see by these examples how closely bound the issue and the conclusion are. Many people have a relatively easy time spotting conclusions, but it's harder for them to pull out the exact issue. This trick of exchanging the conclusion word for "whether" may help you to get started.

Perhaps you are wondering why you should bother pulling out issues when authors and people living their ordinary lives often don't. That's an excellent critical question! Look away from the book and think for a minute whether any of the claims made in chapter 1 might relate to seeing arguments in a "whether" vein.

Any luck? How about the notion of "maybe . . . and maybe not"? If you still don't see the relationship, here is the argument for it:

> **One could argue that** it is crucial for a critical thinker to start out by considering an argument in a balanced, "maybe . . . maybe not" stance. Digging the issue out of an argument brings alternative conclusions to the critical thinker's awareness. For instance, once a person becomes aware that an argument is about "**whether** I'd better spend all day Saturday studying," he or she is closer to the balanced start of "maybe I should study all day, but maybe I shouldn't," rather than being swayed too readily by the conclusion of the argument at hand to study all day. **Therefore,** extracting the issue from the argument is an important part of critical thinking.

Convinced? If not, you're welcome to take issue with the argument.

Conclusions at the Beginning

We're not out of the woods with conclusions yet. Conclusions almost always begin with words like "therefore" and "so" when they occur at the end of an argument. But were you aware that the conclusion of an argument often occurs right at the *start*? When it does, there is no telltale word. (Imagine starting an essay with "therefore"!) Here is a typical example of an argument that starts with its conclusion:

> Eating crackers in bed is a bad idea. First of all, you probably don't need the calories. Moreover, when you turn out the light and lie down, there are all these sharp crumbs which attack you. Then, you have to get up, stumble around in the dark, find the light switch, and either sweep them onto the floor—which is messy—or locate and use a whisk broom and dustpan—which is tedious.

The ideas which follow the opening sentence are all reasons supporting the conclusion that eating crackers in bed is a bad idea. One way to see whether the first statement of any argument is the conclusion is by putting it at the end of the argument, preceded by "therefore," and seeing if that makes sense:

> Eating crackers in bed is a bad idea. First of all, you probably don't need the calories. Moreover, when you turn out the light and lie down, there are all these sharp crumbs which attack you. Then, you have to get up, stumble around in the dark, find the light switch, and either sweep them onto the floor (messy) or get and use a whisk broom and dustpan (tedious). *Therefore, eating crackers in bed is a bad idea.*

And it fits the sense of the argument. Notice what happens if you try this "therefore" test with one of the earlier arguments:

> The weatherman said on the news this morning that it's going to rain today. In fact, when I walked outside I noticed that it was clouding up. I'd better go back and get my umbrella. Therefore the weatherman said on the news this morning that it's going to rain.

It doesn't make sense. The weatherman doesn't say it's going to rain because I'd better go and get my umbrella. (Only a megalomaniac would think so.) That first sentence isn't the conclusion of this argument.

Try your new techniques on Mario's argument, next. Find the sentence you believe to be the conclusion, "test" it if you need to by putting it at the end with "therefore," then see if you can pull out the issue using the term "whether":

> I really deserve to go to the movies tonight. I did several loads of wash (even studying while I was at the laudromat), went to class,

and worked all afternoon. (Therefore, ______________________.)
Mario's conclusion is that ______________________________.
His reason is that ____________________________________.
Mario's issue is whether _________________________________.

The conclusion is almost always found at the very beginning or the end of an argument. In the clearest longer arguments it is found in both places.

VISUALIZE A STRUCTURE

Keep in mind that the basic structure of all arguments great and small is the same. The main issue is brought to a conclusion, with at least one reason to support that conclusion. This structure is really quite simple, and we're using it all the time (fig. 2.1).

The house is not a universal symbol for arguments but provides a way to visualize them. Some form of schematization helps you to see the argument more clearly. This visual analogy is full of helpful figures of speech: A house is called a "structure"; we often refer to well-structured and well-supported arguments. Both houses and arguments can "collapse." It's not good for arguments or houses to "shift" without due notice. Finally, both need to "rest on solid ground."

But why visualize arguments as structures in the first place? If you can readily locate the structure when reading most arguments, by all means don't bother with the visualizations. However, novice critical thinkers are in the habit of seeing the claims in an argument as separate pieces of lumber lying about rather than as parts of a whole. Or they will

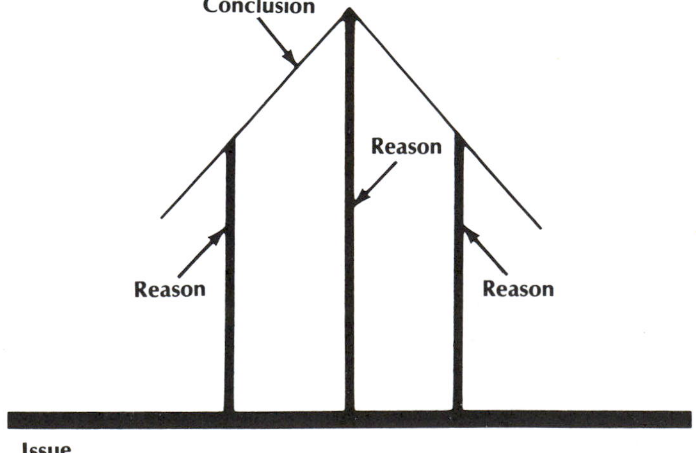

Figure 2.1

read an argument the way one should read a story ("this was said, and then this, and then that"). They thus give each sentence equal importance and often fail to see that certain types of sentences are always going to be more important than others. To overcome this "line by line" habit, *think of yourself as always on a mission in search of the issue, conclusion, and reasons.* If you have to reconstruct the major features of an argument in a visual form, you will be forced to literally see the reasons supporting the conclusion, the way posts hold up the roof of a house.

Let's try this with some day-to-day examples:

ANNIE: Do we need to go to the market this afternoon?
BRUNO: No.
ANNIE: Why not?
BRUNO: We have enough food to last until tomorrow.

The visual structure of this discussion is shown in figure 2.2; the verbal structure is as follows:

ANNIE: Do we need to buy food this afternoon? (*The issue* here is whether Annie and Bruno need to go to the market this afternoon.)
BRUNO: No (*Bruno's conclusion*). We have enough food to last until tomorrow (*Bruno's reason for claiming that they don't need to go to the market*).

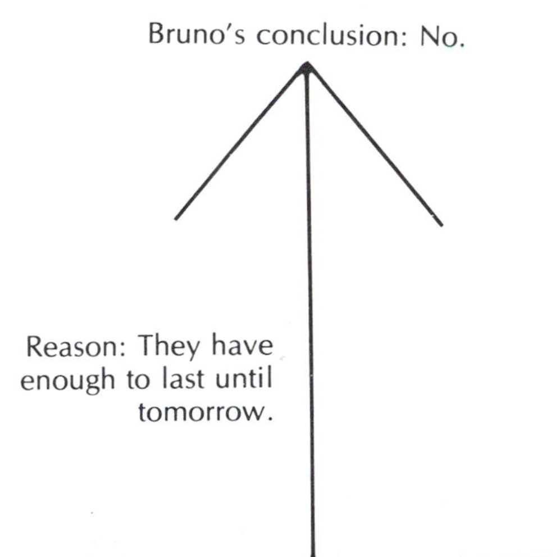

Figure 2.2

Annie raised the *issue* in this case, and Bruno made the argument. Let's continue the dialogue. Can you spot the issue, conclusion, and reason or reasons?

> BRUNO: Well, Annie, do you think we need to go to the market this afternoon?
> ANNIE: No. I'd like to take you out to dinner tonight. Besides, we can always borrow whatever we want from the people next door.

Bruno raised the same issue, and Annie came to the same conclusion that he did (no, we don't need to go to the market); but Annie gave different reasons to support her conclusion. So Annie made a different argument:

> Issue: Do Bruno and Annie need to buy food?
> Annie's conclusion: No.
> Annie's reasons: (1) She wants to take Bruno to dinner; (2) they can borrow whatever they need from the neighbors.

Figure 2.3 is a visual comparison of Annie's and Bruno's arguments. Notice that since the issue of the arguments is the same, the houses are both on the same "block." In fact, thinking of different arguments on a subject as being like different houses on a block isn't a bad way to imagine arguments.

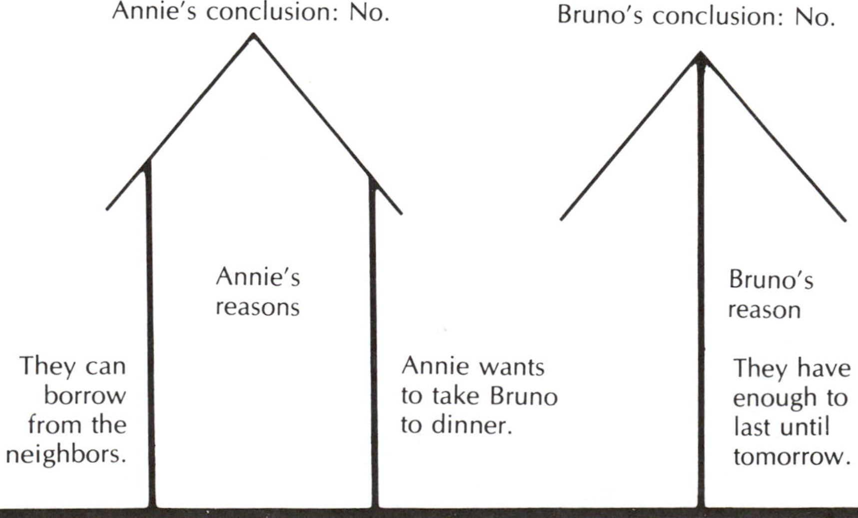

Figure 2.3

Of course, arguing doesn't require two people. One can make an entire argument to oneself, as often happens. Ask yourself whether you need to go to the market today, make a decision (your conclusion), and notice your reasons for deciding the way you did:

> Issue: Do I need to go to the market today?
> Your conclusion: ______________________________________.
> Your reason(s): ______________________________________.

Next, draw a structure to represent your argument.

If you live a simple life, your conclusion was probably a straightforward yes, or no, with one or two reasons. But what if you're not sure, or you think that maybe you'll need to go? Then "not sure" or "maybe" are your conclusions!

Here's an example of a person suffering through life's little aggravations. Hal is really not sure whether he should bother to go to the market, because he can't remember what's in his refrigerator. Then those are his conclusion and reason:

> Hal's issue: Do I need to go to the market today?
> Hal's conclusion: I'm not sure.
> Hal's reason: I can't remember what's in my refrigerator.

People make literally thousands of arguments every day on the question of whether to go to the market. Here is an example of one of a myriad of "maybe" answers:

> Agnes: Let's see . . . do I need to stop by the market today?
> Agnes's conclusion: Maybe.
> Agnes's reasons: If my brother has already gone to the market, then I don't need to go, because he will buy whatever we need. If he hasn't gone yet, then I do need to go.

Agnes has come to a "double" conclusion (maybe yes, maybe no); she has one reason for going and another for not going, but she needs to know an additional *fact* before making her final decision. What is that fact?

She needs to know whether her brother has gone to the market already. Her decision *hinges* on that fact. Agnes's needed fact can be visualized as a beam in the ceiling of the argument structure (see fig. 2.4). If you didn't find this fact on which both arguments hinged, don't worry about it. Examples of facts on which arguments hinge will be presented throughout the book. You'll have plenty of time to catch on.

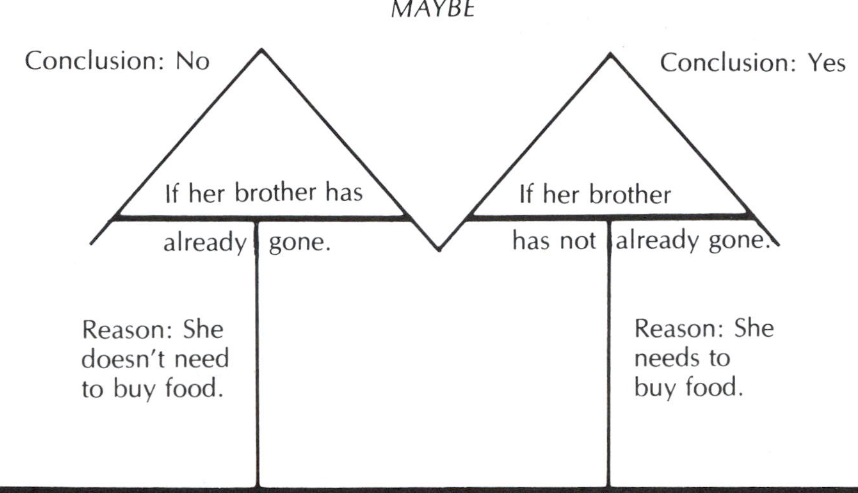

Figure 2.4

DO THE REASONS MAKE SENSE AS REASONS?

It's easy to get careless and just slap down some statement as the reason because it could be a reason in some argument. That won't work here. You have to take a few minutes to think about whether that statement you're writing down is the reason being offered *in the argument at hand.* Think of statements as analogous to pieces of lumber. Just as a board can be made a part of the wall or part of the ceiling, so a statement can be a reason or a conclusion. It depends on what the builder (arguer) decides to do with it.

You might want to say out loud, "The author concludes that . . . because," and see if what you've come up with makes any sense. If it doesn't, out of charity assume first that it may be your fault and look very carefully. Only then can you start wondering about the arguer's carefulness or sanity.

The following is an issue that most of us have to face. Al, the owner of a car 50,000 miles old, inspects the beloved object:

> Gee, I think I'd better get new tires for my car. With these threadbare tires I'm afraid I'll have a blowout on the freeway.

See if you can identify the issue, conclusion, and reason given by the car owner. Diagram the structure first, then analyze the language.

Al's issue is whether ______________________________.
His conclusion is ______________________________.
His reasons are that ______________________________.

If you determined that the issue is whether Al should get new tires and his conclusion was yes; and if you wrote that his reason was that he's afraid that with his threadbare tires he'll have a blowout on the freeway, you've done well. If you decided that he gave two reasons, that his tires were threadbare and that he was afraid that he'd have a blowout, that's even better. But if you got it wrong, let's figure out how you can avoid the mistake in the future.

What, for example, if you had this:

Al's issue: Whether with his threadbare tires he'll have a blowout on the freeway.
Al's conclusion: Yes.
Al's reason is that he thinks he'd better get new tires for his car.

Would Al have a blowout *because he thinks* he'd better get new tires? That would be a cosmic injustice to careful car owners; that's not Al's reasoning. You have to spend a couple of minutes pondering whether the reason makes sense. Say to yourself "Is that *really* the reason?" Most people who misidentify the reason just haven't stopped long enough to think it through.

SOME BOOK TITLES ARE CONCLUSIONS

Book titles offer the first clues about what a book will argue. The title of a book or article may give just the general topic, as opposed to specifying an issue within that topic. Let's inspect a few topic titles. Take, for example, a book entitled *Execution.* Notice that the issue is not clear: Is it a book about the incidence of execution, its rightfulness or wrongfulness, an evaluation of state-approved or gangland-style, or some bizarre how-to book? We'd have to look at the table of contents to see. Other topic titles: *On History, The Germans.* Here again, while the titles tell us the overall topic, we have no idea what the authors are concluding about history or about the Germans. For a precise issue, we must dig out an author's main conclusion and then place "whether" in front. In a well-written book, we need not dig deeply.

Often the title of a book or article contains the author's overall conclusion. When you pull the issues out of these title-conclusions it helps you to see that conclusions other than the ones the authors suggest are quite possible. Consider these examples: *You Can't Spoil Your Baby; I'm*

O.K.—You're O.K.; India: A Wounded Civilization; The Disappearance of Childhood; Winning Through Intimidation; or *The Criminal as Victim.*

In these cases we know what the authors have concluded, but not why they have done so. From the last title we can infer that the author has concluded that the criminal is a victim, whereby we can helpfully turn this around to the issue of whether the criminal is a victim. But we don't yet know the author's argument. Why is the criminal a victim? Will the argument be that it's because of the criminal's environment or genetic makeup or some other cause? The answer to that question will have to come as a result of browsing through the book or reading it.

WHEN YOU WRITE ABOUT SEVERAL RELATED ISSUES

We will deal at length with complex arguments in chapter 10, but start to familiarize yourself with the following phrases for the main issue:

The central question that must now be asked **is** . . .
In my opinion, **the foremost issue is** . . .
The **fundamental problem** that we must first solve **is** . . .

Once the main issue has been discussed, the reader must somehow be alerted that a second issue is going to be raised. For the issue that's second in importance (or for the one that is dealt with next), a paragraph could begin with the following:

There is **a second problem.**
Subordinate to this **main issue is the question whether . . .**

Each time the issue changes, the reader should be alerted:

There is still **a third difficulty.**
Of **further** importance is the **question whether . . .**

SUMMARY

There are three basic features of argumentation in the strict sense: *An issue is brought to a conclusion with the support of at least one reason.* These basic features may appear anywhere in an argument. Therefore the critical thinker must actively seek them out by asking questions.

What is the author trying to have me think or do? That is, what is the author's conclusion? Tip-off terms may occur at the end of the paragraph: "therefore," "in conclusion," "to summarize." If not, the conclusion may well be at the beginning.

What is the exact issue? Try replacing the "therefore" word with "whether."

What are the reasons? If the word "reason" doesn't appear, look for "because"; whatever occurs after that word is a reason. See if it makes sense as a reason that supports the conclusion.

If you can't find these telltale terms, and you know that the author is driving home a point, see if any of these synonyms is doing the work:

THEREFORE	**BECAUSE**
in short	since
so	for (before a clause)
it follows that	for the reason that
it is believed that	the source is
shows that	
indicates that	
proves that	
we may conclude that	
necessitates	

Don't forget to check for the conclusion at the beginning.

DISTINCTIONS

Arguments involve decisions of two sorts: what to do and what to think. The examples in this chapter have been about what to do in day-to-day life. The arguments which follow are all of the other sort, dealing with what to think. Obviously, there is considerable overlap between what one does and what one thinks, but the general distinction is useful. Some students will have more trouble with arguments about what to think. If you are one of them, review the first part of this chapter, keeping in mind that the structure is the same in both types of argument.

Another distinction regarding arguments is between those that make claims about what *is* the case and those that make claims about what *should be* the case. While there are a few examples of purely factual or purely directive arguments, much argumentation that at first seems purely factual is actually directive as well. Does this chapter, for example, argue (in the loose sense) about what the basic features of formal argument *are*, or does it direct you on what they *should* be? Both, actually.

EXERCISES

1. The following are brief arguments about human nature expressed clearly and cleverly. Whether you agree or disagree, you might become intrigued by them.

a. People often think they are in love when they are not: the excitement of an intrigue, the emotional flutter of gallantry, natural delight in being loved, and the difficulty of saying no, all these conspire to persuade them that they are feeling passionate when they are merely being flirtatious.[1]

(1) Diagram the structure.
(2) Analyze the language.
The issue here is whether ______________________________.
The author concludes that ______________________________.
His reasons for making this argument are ______________________________.
The issue is whether people often wrongly think they are in love. **The author concludes that this is the case. His reasons are that** people confuse the excitement of an intrigue, the emotional flutter of gallantry, natural delight in being loved, and the difficulty of saying no for being in love (feeling passionate).

The language of your analysis doubtless varied somewhat from that above. Don't be concerned, as long as you have stated your answers in complete, grammatical sentences and have used "issue," "reason," and "conclusion" for the correct ideas. Study the phrasing that is in boldface, however. Repeat it a number of times, and think about copying it in your essays to expand your repertoire of critical thinking phrases. You might even copy the language used in the foregoing example when writing out the exercise which follows.

b. People hate injustice, not because it is inherently wrong, but because of the harm it does them.[2]

(1) Diagram the structure.
(2) Analyze the language. Provide a description of the basics, being careful to use the language of argument exemplified in boldface type. When you give the reason, be sure to say, "The reason is **that.**" Never write, "The reason is because"; it is redundant.

It would be all right to ignore the statement, "It [injustice] is inherently wrong." You could also draw a falling wall-beam (a negation symbol is printed over it) to indicate that the author alleges that it is *not* the reason that people hate injustice (see fig. 2.5).

Just be certain that you did not put down, "Injustice is inherently wrong" as the *author's* reason, even though it might be your reason and might be true. One of the most important tasks is to separate your opinion from that of the person who is presenting an argument.

c. One of the most important things you must do as a critical thinker is to be aware of how your opinion differs from that of the person who is presenting you an argument. Otherwise, you will not learn this new opinion.

(1) Diagram the structure.
(2) Analyze the language.
The writer proposes the issue whether one of the most important things that you must do as a critical thinker is to distinguish your opinion from that of the person who is presenting an argument, **concluding that** this is the case, and **giving the reason that** otherwise you will not learn this new opinion. Notice that even though the reason contains a "not," it *still* is the author's reason, unilke the "injustice" example before it, in which the author was telling something that was *not* his reason.

Rule: If the word "not" goes in front of the word "because" or "reason," then it's *not the reason.* Otherwise, it is the reason. For example: He rewrote his essay not because he had to, but because he did not want to turn in shoddy work ("because he did not want to turn in shoddy work" being the reason argued).

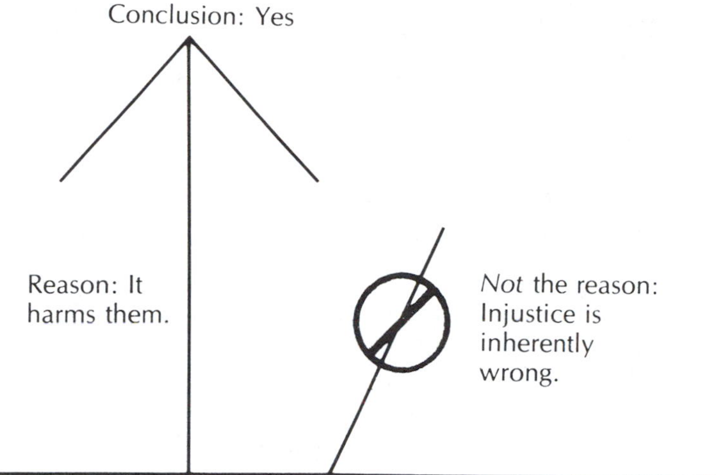

Figure 2.5

Mull over this distinction until it makes sense to you.

d. When we have grown tired of loving, we are delighted at the other's unfaithfulness, for that releases us from having to be faithful.[3]

Hint: Watch the issue. Don't make it broader than the arguer does.
(1) Diagram the structure.
(2) Analyze the language.
The issue under discussion is whether we are delighted at the other's unfaithfulness when we have grown tired of loving. **The author concludes in the affirmative, reasoning that** it releases us from having to be faithful. (Your statement of the author's issue must include "when we have grown tired of loving." Otherwise you are stating that the author is claiming that we generally delight in others' unfaithfulness to us. The author has, however, **qualified his statement.**)

2. You're on your own! Identify the issue, reason, and conclusion, using the pictorial structure if it helps.
   a. We should not take offense when people hide the truth from us, since so often we hide it from ourselves.[4]

(1) Diagram the structure.
(2) Analyze the language.
The issue at hand is whether ______________________________.
The author concludes that ______________________________.
The reason offered is that ______________________________.

   b. Little is needed to make a wise man happy, but nothing can content a fool. That is why nearly all men are miserable.[5]
   c. I don't trust him. We're friends.[6]

Is this last example a strict argument or just two factual claims side by side? Why?

3. Which of the following are loose arguments; which are strict?
   a. I saw him tiptoe across the lawn and steal softly into the house. It was broad daylight.
   b. Since I'm not in the business of giving advice, I refused to tell him which career to choose.
   c. When the stock market is down, buy more stock. When it's up, sell.
   d. Thinking about how to spend your time most efficiently is of vital importance.
   e. Thinking about how to spend your time most efficiently is of vital importance, because that's the only way you'll accomplish your major goals in life.

   Answers: a. two loose arguments (just two claims, one not the reason for the other); b. strict argument; c. two loose arguments; d. loose argument; e. strict argument

4. What are the issue, conclusion, and reason(s) in the following two arguments?

1

Should there be a law requiring motorcyclists to wear helmets? Many motorcyclists would argue "No." They object to a helmet law because the helmet reduces peripheral vision and hearing acuity. Another reason is that helmets interfere with the freedom of being completely exposed to the elements.

2

Motorcycle accidents cause more than four thousand deaths and tens of thousands of brain injuries each year in the United States. In California alone $60 million to $100 million is taken from the public purse each year to pay medical bills of riders injured while they were not wearing helmets. So while some motorcyclists say "Let those who ride decide," I would argue that "Those who pay should have the final say," a helmet law.

READINGS

1. Should we consider the welfare (interests) of animals as equal to that of humans? While admitting that "this suggestion may at first seem bizarre," Peter Singer makes a persuasive argument. What is his basic argument?

The capacity for suffering and enjoying things is a prerequisite to having interests at all, a condition that must be satisfied before we can speak of interests in any meaningful way. It would be nonsense to say that it was not in the interests of a stone to be kicked along the road by a schoolboy. A stone does not have interests because it cannot suffer. Nothing that we can do to it could possibly make any difference to its welfare. A mouse, on the other hand, does have an interest in not being tormented, because it will suffer if it is.

If a being suffers, there can be no moral justification for refusing to take that suffering into consideration. No matter what the nature of the being, the principle of equality requires that its suffering be counted equally with the like suffering—insofar as rough comparisons can be made—of any other being . . . .

Racists violate the principle of equality by giving greater weight to the interests of members of their own race when there is a clash between their interests and the interests of those of another race. White racists do not accept that pain is as bad when it is felt by blacks as when it is felt by whites. Similarly, those I would call "specieists" give greater weight to the interests of members of their own species where there is a clash between their interests and the interests of those of other species. Human specieists do not accept that pain is as bad when it is felt by pigs or mice as when it is felt by humans.

That, then, is really the whole of the argument for extending the principle of equality to nonhuman animals.[7]

Analyze Singer's argument:
Singer raises the issue whether ______________________________.
He argues (concludes) that ______________________________.
because ______________________________.

2. Philosopher Paul Weiss became curious about the deep love many people feel for sports. The book *Sport: A Philosophic Inquiry* was the result. Keep the following in mind as you read this excerpt from Weiss's book:
   a. Two of these paragraphs entail almost all factual claims; the third contains an argument. Which is which?
   b. One way to deal with a lot of closely related questions is to summarize them into one "umbrella" question.
   c. Look for the conclusion and then work backwards (a good ploy most of the time).

Athletes usually submit themselves, often with enthusiasm, rarely with reluctance, to long periods of training. They do not seem to mind having to engage repeatedly in dull exercises and tedious practice sessions. Nor do they seem to take amiss the need to control their appetites, even those that are imperious and insistent. Willingly, athletes sacrifice opportunities to be lax, give up occasions to be irresponsible, and put aside a desire simply to enjoy themselves. At times they risk injury, and in some cases death. Fatigue is a familiar. Sooner or later every one of them comes to know . . . defeat, and perhaps humiliation. [The athlete's] days are numbered, successes rarely momentous, and glories short-lived; [one] works hard and long to prepare . . . for what may end in dismal failure. Why?

Why are athletes ready to give up so much that is desirable to accept what involves a good deal of wasted motion and boredom? Why are they willing to risk making their inadequacies evident, instead of enjoying the struggle of others from afar, or instead of plunging into a game without concern for how they might fare? Why do they subject themselves to the demands of a severe disciplining? Why are they so ready to practice self-denial or to sacrifice their interest in other pursuits to prepare themselves for what may prove disastrous? Why are they so prone to accept advice, often from [others] not nearly so competent as they themselves are? Strong, with more than the normal amount of pride and impulsiveness, why do they docilely listen to criticism which is not infrequently phrased in brutal or scathing terms?

These questions are not often asked. But unless they are, we will not learn what it is that the athlete wants or . . . should get. The answer that I think should be accepted—[is that] sport attracts because it offers a superb occasion for enabling young [people] to be perfected . . . to have fine functioning bodies and thereby reveal [one dimension of what humans] can be and do . . . .[8]

Analyze Weiss's argument.

NOTES

[1]LaRochefoucauld, *Maxims,* trans. Leonard Tancock (New York: Penguin Books, 1981), p. 74.

[2]*Ibid.,* p. 117.

[3]*Ibid.*

[4]*Ibid.,* p. 105.

[5]*Ibid.,* p. 108.

[6]Bertolt Brecht, quoted in Robert Byrne, ed., *The 637 Best Things Anybody Ever Said* (New York: Ballantine Books, a division of Random House, Inc., 1982).

[7]Peter Singer, *Practical Ethics* (New York: Cambridge University Press, 1980), pp. 50–51.

[8]Paul Weiss, *Sport: A Philosophic Inquiry* (n.p.: Southern Illinois University Press, 1969), pp. 18–19.

CHAPTER THREE

ALTERNATIVE ARGUMENTS

The basic structure of argument consists of issue, conclusion, and reasons—three of the twelve basics. You have also been alerted to a fourth fundamental feature, distinction. That leaves eight. At this point, there is no "correct" next move. Having discovered the three basics in any argument, you could proceed to consider any of the remaining features next. You might, for example, immediately proceed to generate alternative arguments (fig. 3.1); or you might pursue one of the other areas of argument shown in figure 3.2. These will be thoroughly discussed in chapters 4 through 7.

Alternative arguments are presented next because they give you a lot to work with. The novice critical thinker, when faced with an argument to critique, often worries, "I can't think of anything to say." In a few weeks you will suffer from the opposite problem, wondering which of many approaches to take.

Most important, alternative arguments broaden your perspective on the issue to a greater extent than the other remaining tools. Ultimately you will come to see how **critical thinking is consideration of alternative arguments in light of their evidence.**

Figure 3.1. Generating alternative arguments.

QUICK STARTS

Quick Start 1

The easiest way to get a second argument on an issue is to *oppose the conclusion* of the first and support that opposite conclusion with a reason:

> First argument: Students shouldn't underline in their textbooks, because they can sell them back to the bookstore for more money when the books have no writing in them.
>
> Second argument (oppose conclusion of first and back up with a reason): Students should underline in their textbooks, because doing so will help them to get better grades.

Now you try. Think up a strict argument, then oppose it.

Quick Start 2

Another easy way to come up with a second argument is to *oppose the conclusion and oppose a reason* or reasons offered by the first:

> First argument: Students shouldn't underline in their textbooks, because they can sell them back to the bookstore for more money when the books have no writing in them.
>
> Second argument (oppose first conclusion and its reason): Students should underline in their textbooks, because once they've written

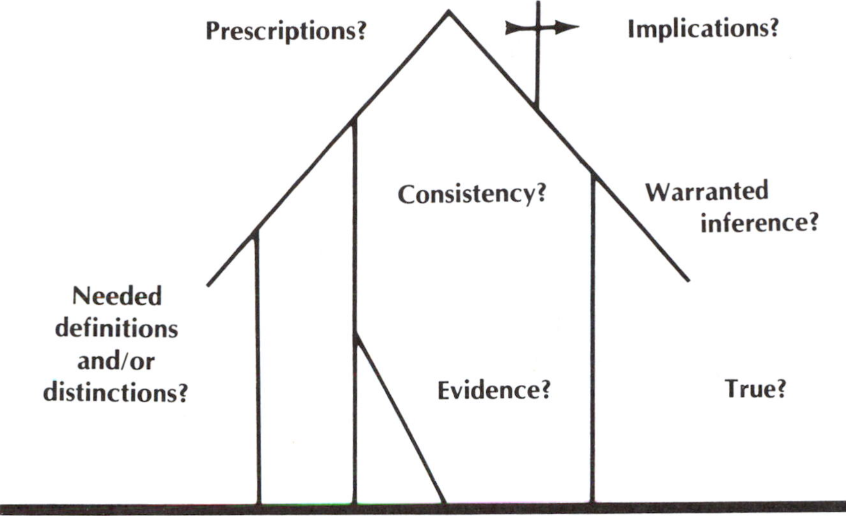

Figure 3.2

their names in them, the bookstore buys them back at the same used price whether the students underline in them or not.

If the reasons for the foregoing arguments are true, questions still remain. For instance, we're still faced with the question whether students should write their *names* in their textbooks. But the issue has expanded, and the argument is making progress.

It would mean even more progress if the arguments could "speak directly to one another." Here, for instance, if underlining tends to help students get better grades (but how much better), should students go for better grades over a bigger refund (but how big is the refund)? We need to engage these arguments directly with one another to make the most enlightened decision about underlining textbooks. In the next two sections you'll see how to get arguments directly engaged in this way.

FACTORS FOR, FACTORS AGAINST

Say that someone argues that grades should be abolished because they create bad feelings in students who get poor marks. If a school were seriously considering eliminating grades, then students, school administrators, teachers, and even businesses would have to consider a great

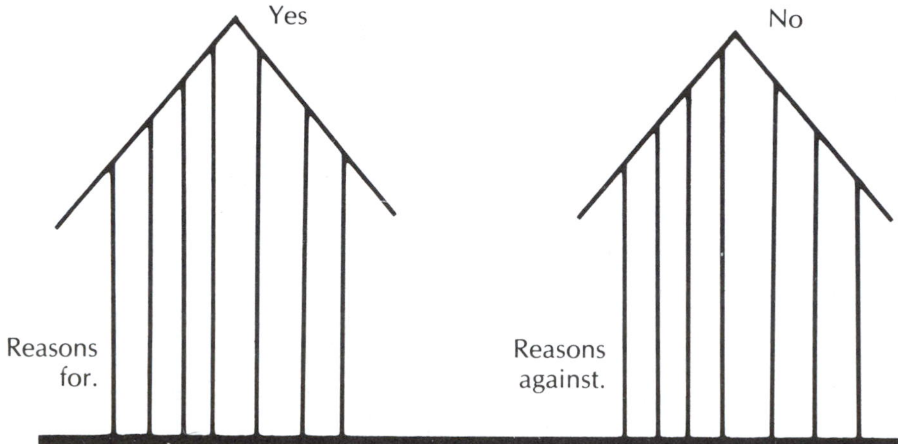

Issue: Whether grades should be abolished.

Figure 3.3

many factors before being in favor of it. Brainstorm for a few minutes, listing as many factors as you can in favor of abolishing grades, and then do the same against the idea. Don't forget to include favorable and unfavorable factors from the point of view of nonstudents. For the moment, put down everything you can think of, no matter how zany it sounds.

In thinking up these factors, you will be generating *reasons* which you could use in arguments for and against grades (see fig. 3.3).

Now do the same for underlining in textbooks.

Winnow Out the Strongest Reasons

Do not censor yourself in coming up with factors, because sometimes a wild idea can lead you by association to a very good idea. In fact, sometimes the wild idea, upon further reflection, *is* a good idea. Many ideas considered nonsense in one century become common sense in the next.*

To prevent an argument from becoming unwieldy, it is best to reduce both sets of factors to what, in your opinion, are the two or three strongest, most convincing reasons. If your wilder idea happens to convince you, by all means use it, and make it a convincing reason for others.

*Instances of ideas which when propounded seemed outlandish to most, but later drew millions of adherents: Christianity, Marxism, Einstein's theory of relativity (a wild idea winning general acceptance within twenty years, rather than a hundred); Freudian notions of the unconscious, neurosis, and repression; equality of the sexes.

ENGULF AND DEVOUR

Here is a wonderful three-part technique for developing a sophisticated argument. Its "point, counter-point, point" structure really engages opposing arguments:

1. Strongest reasons for First, you make the strongest case you can for some position. First argue for, say, the importance of grades (or of an athletics requirement or capital punishment), offering your strongest reasons in support of this position.

2. Strongest reasons against Then you argue against grades, offering the strongest reasons you can to abolish grades (athletics requirements, capital punishment).

3. Engulf and devour the second argument Taking the first position again, you argue that **even granting** the truth of the reasons offered in this second argument, say, against grades, the argument for grades is stronger because . . . .

"Engulf and devour" is a very powerful form of argumentation because the arguer acknowledges the opposing point of view at its best and goes on to show how the first argument is still better. The following argument in favor of brainstorming illustrates "engulf and devour."

1. Strongest reasons for One of the best ways to get critical material is to play around with an argument, generating as many factors favorable or unfavorable to it as one can. Generating factors also helps the critical thinker to consider an issue in broad perspective, from many angles.

2. Strongest reasons against **On the other hand, one could argue that** this method of generating arguments is inadvisable because it is dishonest. The honest approach would be to gather evidence before ever entertaining a factor as part of an argument. For instance, **according to this argument**, one should gather statistics on how many students have performed better in ungraded courses than graded before ever alleging that students do better in ungraded courses as a factor in favor of abolishing grades.

3. Engulf and devour the second argument **Yet even granting that** honesty in making arguments is necessary, it is possible to be honest and still to generate playfully as much of an argument as possible. One remains honest throughout this endeavor by realizing that the ideas so generated are exploratory, not final. And it is arguable that surveying the whole landscape of factors, rather than limiting oneself to an immediately demonstrable few, will result in a fuller and, therefore, more honest argument. **It is, in fact, arguable whether** one could come up with definitive statistics showing that students do better in ungraded courses. **Moreover, accepting that the second argument offered that** evidence plays a vital role in finally deciding whether a factor is a strong reason for accepting an argument, **the fact remains that** most critical thinkers, scientists included, advance by making an imaginative leap beyond the evidence at hand and then looking to see if evidence exists in support of the new idea. In sum, with arguments as well as in many areas of life, it is better to leap before you look.

You can see that this three-part argument is a lot stronger than the first part of the argument alone.

One final note: Engulf and devour is a two-way treat. Someone might come along saying "**even granting all that has been said** about leaping before one looks, **still,** careful investigation should precede all argumentation **because,**" thus engulfing and devouring this example whole!

If It's Better, Accept It

If in the course of making a strong opposing argument the arguer becomes convinced of the opposing argument, the arguer has learned something. There should be no shame in that, only in obtusely refusing to budge from one's original position in the teeth of better reasons. (See chapter 11 for a distinction between deliberation, which allows you to gracefully embrace the opposite argument, and debate, which prohibits you from accepting the opposite argument under pain of "losing the debate.")

If you are in the middle of writing a paper and convince yourself of the opposite argument, just switch the placement of the argument and counterargument, enabling whatever position can engulf and devour to do so.

Of course, that second argument may persuade you intellectually while making you uneasy emotionally. Remember that in the interests of balance you can accept an argument provisionally—no cost, no obligation to act on it today.

ONE BIG FACTOR AGAINST

In some cases one argument can engulf another, but many times this is not possible. You can't in conscience grant the truth of all of the reasons in an opposing argument. So engulfing is out. The next best approach is to try to think up the *strongest possible reason against* the argument. Again, generate a number of *factors against* a position and then winnow out the one or two most likely to change the opinion of a person who believed the position.

Take the issue of grade abolition. Say that someone has presented two strong factors in favor of abolition: (1) that many people would actually try harder, no longer feeling incompetent because of bad grades and (2) that everyone would work for the correct reason, that is, the value of learning, rather than for an extrinsic reward.

Now, what is the strongest reason that can come up against those reasons? Another way of putting it is to ask, "What is the main reason that grades exist?" You may have thought of a better answer, but one answer is that grades are supposed to let both the individual and society (employers, graduate schools, etc.) know what level of skill an individual has attained in a given subject. This is, then, a factor in favor of grades. In countering the argument against grades, one could say:

> **However, in arguing that** grades should be abolished, **the author has failed to take the problem of** standards of preparedness **into account.**

or

> **The proponents of** grade abolition **must address the difficult necessity of** distinguishing those who are skilled from those who are not skilled in a subject.

Tactfully raising these important problems for the arguer is doing the arguer a great favor.

COUNTEREXAMPLE

This tack, of coming up with one significant exception, works especially well on arguments that at first seem so airtight as to be inevitable. Consider this argument about boredom:

> It's plain that boredom results from outside stimuli which are dull, repetitious, or tedious. People become bored because they are in such an environment.

Who could fight that argument? We've all been in such situations, and it's obvious that people get bored because they're in boring situations. But wait—just fool around trying to remember whether you've been in situations where boredom *can't* have occurred because of dull, outside stimuli. Rack your brain for a few minutes. Any ideas? If not, here's one approach. Think of any situations in which one person has been bored and another *hasn't*? We're searching for any exceptions to the claim that boredom has to come from dull, outside stimuli. Any situation in which some people get bored and others don't can be used to argue against the position that boring situations are just "out there" in the same way that boiling water is "out there" on the stove.

If you can think up such an exceptional case, you can use it to back up your counterargument:

> **On the contrary, one could argue that** boredom **does not result** from outside stimuli which are dull, repetitious, or tedious. **For instance,** ____.

For instance, there are many people who would find a lecture on thermodynamics boring, while others would find it quite interesting.

Finding such exceptions can be a revelation. If you have always believed that a boring situation came from the outside world, attacked, and bored you, then you should now feel puzzled, wondering just how people do get bored. That puzzlement is good. It will lead you to deepen your awareness on the subject.

ARGUE (ALONE) THAT THE FIRST POSITION'S REASONS ARE NO GOOD

The first argument's reasons may be false, or they may be true but too flimsy to support the conclusion. Either of these factors is ruinous to an argument. Each will be dealt with at length: truth of reasons in chapter 5 and strength of reasons in chapters 4, 5, 12, and 13.

Examples of language used to criticize reasons:

> **It has been claimed that** the abolition of grades would result in greater efforts on the part of many students. **This argument does not hold because its reason is simply untrue. It is not the case that** students would try harder; if anything, a lot of students would stop trying entirely.

Taking the first argument's reasons head-on is a favored strategy when you are alone and trying to decide whether to accept an argument. It's easy to run the reasons through one's experience and past reasoning on the issue, coming to a decision. But accusing reasons of being false or flimsy is the least-favored method when arguing with someone else. The reason is due to the complexity of the human mind. Take the example of grades. The person who is convinced that grades should be abolished is probably already convinced of a lot of other things as well, perhaps that people are basically intellectually curious and that the carrot of academic enjoyment is better than the stick of bad grades. These other, deeper convictions beneath the argument at hand are called *assumptions* and are discussed in chapter 6. A person's reasons for accepting an argument are normally much more complicated than the argument at hand would lead one to believe. In addition, people like what they believe, and feel a personal stake in it.

The complexity of human reason and the commitment to belief are two reasons why "engulf and devour" is such a powerful argumentative tool. When it can be used, it leaves all the apparatus of the person's beliefs intact, while enlarging them.*

TIME OUT FOR FACT-FINDING OR EXPERIMENTATION

You probably realized while reading the example of grade abolition that you had no statistics that would help you to decide whether, in fact, abolishing grades would help students to work harder or not. You doubtless have your suspicions about the matter, but if you're arguing with someone of opposite suspicions, you're stuck.

One approach would be to suggest researching for past or present cases in which schools have abolished grades:

> **The author has argued that** the elimination of grades will improve student efforts. **If we are to seriously entertain this possibility, thorough research** of the effect of grade abolition on other schools similar to ours **must be undertaken.**

or

> **More facts must be gathered on the question whether . . . before it can be decided.**

When past and present cases cannot be found, an arguer can call for experimentation. Consider these examples:

> **Only experimentation will decide the question whether** searching students on high school campuses for weapons will reduce the incidence of violence.

*Big factor and significant exception also tend to enlarge the perspective of the other side, although not to as great an extent.

At the moment, the answer remains controversial. **It might be resolved by further experimentation.**

Notice that the second writer has decided to be more cautious about the role experimentation will play in deciding the issue at hand.

BALANCE AND BELIEF

If you happen to agree with an argument, it's going to sound terrific. If you violently disagree, an argument will sound like it's full of holes and just terrible. Both of these tendencies are hard on balance, and mean that everyone has to work to be tougher on arguments with which they already agree, more tender with those they initially feel opposed to. This may seem obvious, but it often gets lost in the flush of argument.

Don't infer that openness to counterarguments means to accept all arguments as equal. That would lead to *relativism,* the view that there is no ultimate truth. Openness to counterarguments is meant to defend against a different danger, that of *dogmatism,* the belief that one already has all the truth to be known on a subject. Dogmatism is the refusal to entertain a different point of view.

There is an intermediate, balanced view which has aided material as well as social progress—*progressivism.* It holds that the truth is real and that, thanks to the community of thinkers, we're getting closer to it on many issues. At the heart of progressivism is a willingness always to entertain counterarguments, even on positions on which near-certainty is felt.

The distinction among these three beliefs is crucial. As figure 3.4 indicates, relativism makes fresh information to be of little consequence, and dogmatism locks it out.

Obviously, you do not have to agree.

I can't think of any alternatives beyond these three positions, but can you?

LOGOPHOBIA, THE FEAR OF ARGUING

If you slink away from an argument, it's often from fear that the conclusion is true. If that conclusion is right, you may feel that it could do violence to one or more of your deeply felt beliefs—and therefore violence could be done to *you*! So in a sheer panic of self-protection, you retreat.

Now, one can remain in permanent retreat or make a comeback—that is, get back into balance—either to make a counterargument or to defer making one. Let's make the case for the comeback. (You may have

Progressivism: The truth is real, and we're on a never-ending journey towards it.

Truth

Dogmatism: The belief that one has already arrived at the truth and can rest, complacently asserting that no differing view matters.

Truth

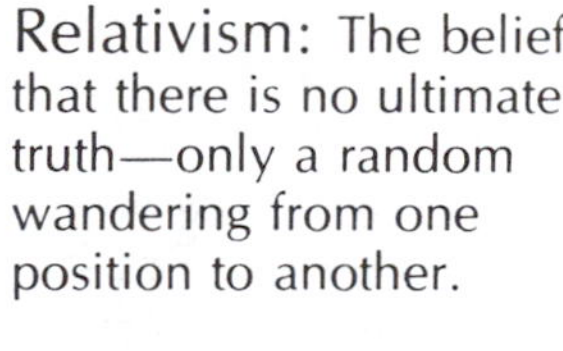

Relativism: The belief that there is no ultimate truth—only a random wandering from one position to another.

Figure 3.4

noticed that the foregoing paragraph was an argument in favor of retreating.) Imagine a second "you" talking to the "you" crouching in a corner:

> Look, you really should face up to this argument. No matter what happens, you stand to win, whether you become convinced by the argument or not.
>
> Say that you give the argument your most sincere efforts but aren't convinced. Chances are that you've seen flaws in it that will help you to find more points to make your original belief even stronger. So by looking at a counterargument you have enriched your original argument.
>
> On the other hand, assume that after giving the argument your sincerest efforts you find that you do become persuaded by that argument. You can easily define your experience as one of *changing* your beliefs as if having had violence done to your old belief. After all, the old belief isn't dead—as long as you leave yourself open to persuasion, you can take back your old belief any time you decide that it is more convincing to you.
>
> And just as violence is not really done to the belief, violence is not really done to you. It just seems that violence is going to be done to you, because you are experiencing fear that such a big belief change will turn you into an unknown quantity, maybe even cause you to lose your identity. It's true that your beliefs are an important part of you, but you are, in fact, more than the sum of your beliefs; you are a reasoning, feeling, many-faceted human being. And rather than the new belief having a power of its own that changes you, *you,* in fact, have been in charge all along, changing your belief! However, if you continue to hide over there, not making an informed choice between the belief you have and this one, you can hardly consider yourself in charge.
>
> Remember, too, that you can always accept an argument *provisionally*—in fact you should. You can think, "I can't beat that argument at the moment, so I'll accept it for the time being. But I'm still uneasy with it, so I certainly won't act on it yet. But now I'm fascinated, so I will definitely keep thinking about it, and look for arguments others have made on the issue." Temporary acceptance pending further thought will not force you out into the street to act on that belief.

Welcome All Comers

If we can acquire the habit of seeing arguments as opportunities to acquire wisdom, with no possibility of "losing" an argument since we always "win" insight, it will be easy to cultivate a spirit of welcome for any ideas. Then no argument need scare us off—at least not for long. Or would you like to make the opposite argument? All you have to do is to turn the conclusion around, claiming "No, there are some positions that should never even be considered. My reason(s) for saying this are that ___________. For instance (strongest exception), ___________.

Example of a Horrifying Issue

What assertion could we practice on that would displease nearly everyone? How about the argument that torture is right under certain circumstances? The most offensive argument on the subject would probably be that we should be constantly torturing one another. But one couldn't construct a good foundation for that conclusion. I'll make do by arguing that torture under a few circumstances is right. Note that this argument is as persuasive as possible because the **strongest case** has been taken.

> Torture is not only right but a positive obligation in certain very limited circumstances. By "torture" I mean the willful infliction of physical pain on another, unwilling person.

delimit scope of argument definition

> The decison to torture another person is a grievous one. I would rule out almost all cases of torture as inhumane and therefore highly immoral. Yet consider this frightening scenario: A man has hidden a plutonium bomb somewhere in New York City. When captured, the man claims that the bomb will go off in half an hour, that all New Yorkers deserve to die, and that he will not tell where the bomb is.

emphasize limited acceptability

strongest case: death to millions over pain to one

> With millions of lives at stake, the police sergeant surely has the right to apply a bit of pressure, perhaps starting with the delicate fold of skin between the man's thumb and index finger and increasing the man's pain until he reveals the bomb's location.

strongest case: recommend least pain necessary

> In fact, torture of this man will have the effect of saving his life as well as the lives the millions held in jeopardy. But consider this statement: "The right of one person to be free of pain is greater than the right of millions, even if that one person would take the lives of those millions of people." Doesn't that sound wrong? The right of many people to live is in fact greater than the right of one person to be temporarily free of pain, especially if that one person has put the millions in jeopardy.

strongest case, *even for man tortured!*

By "strongest case" you should recognize the significant exception, the most persuasive example that you can imagine. Then to respond to the argument, you might keep that strongest case in mind and generate an argument "engulfing and devouring"—claiming why, even in that strongest case, torture would still be wrong. For example,

> Don't accept even this compelling case. Once torture is permitted, where will the line be drawn? Should we torture one person who even *says* she's got a plutonium bomb and will hurt three people with it?

(See? A strong case in the opposite direction.)

Use Uneasiness to Generate Alternatives

If you dislike both the argument and the counterargument, use that dislike to propel yourself into creating alternative ways of dealing with an issue. In the case of a terrorist with a bomb, aren't the alternatives quite limited? Perhaps, but it would be better to assume that the alternatives are *unlimited.* Otherwise we wouldn't bother to think up alternatives, possibly missing some very important solutions to our problems. For example, consider how the Dutch have dealt with the terrorism that plagued their country several years ago. The terrorists were a few of the Moluccan immigrants to Holland from their islands near Indonesia. They wanted independence for their islands, which were once under Dutch rule but overtaken by Indonesia in the 1950s. In the late 1970s the Dutch Moluccans hijacked trains and "executed" a number of people until the government came up with a unique alternative. Why not send some Moluccans back to visit their islands? First, they would see that their quarrel was with Indonesia, not Holland. Second, life in Holland compares very favorably with life in the Moluccas, so they would not even want to go back to live in the Moluccas. The Dutch paid the fare for perhaps 10 percent of the 40,000 Moluccans living in Holland. The terrorism has stopped.[1]

Obviously, this won't work in a number of other terrorist hot spots. But maybe *some as yet unthought alternative* would.

MISCELLANEOUS ADVICE

When you hear an argument, think *"Yes, maybe so, but."* For the fun of it try to generate a counterargument or at least some reasons why the argument at hand may not be complete.

> *Try to think of instances that don't fit the argument.* Take the reason and imagine some exception. *Or make a strong opposite case.*
> *Try to imagine what the person is arguing—both for and against.*

Ask yourself *whether the argument needs more* support in the form of *evidence or reasons;* perhaps the argument needs the support of different reasons. Don't forget that there are times when the opposite case is better just because it's closer to the truth.

SUMMARY

The following tactics were discussed in this chapter:

1. *Quick starts:* Oppose the conclusion, come up with a reason; oppose the conclusion and reason(s).
2. *Factors for and against:* Brainstorm for as many factors as possible on either side, then winnow them down to the best few.
3. *Engulf and devour:* Accept the opposing argument, offering more powerful reasons to accept your argument.
4. *A big factor, a significant exception, the strongest case:* A search for missing elements that the arguer has not taken into account.
5. *Argue that the first position's reasons are no good:* Reasons are false or flimsy.
6. *Call for more factual evidence or for experimentation.*

Although these are different approaches, they can overlap.

EXERCISES

1. Use one of the quick start techniques on each of these arguments:
   a. Everyone should buy a few clothes every year because wearing something different adds spice to life.
   b. Fraternities and sororities are clubs whose sole purpose is to make their members feel superior to outsiders. These clubs should be banned from college campuses.
2. Factors for, factors against:
   a. Generate five reasons in favor of a flat, 15% federal income tax for every person and every business; then imagine five reasons against such an idea. Winnow the reasons on each side to two, then choose the strongest, explaining why it is strongest.
   b. Think of alternative ways, even zany ones, to tax people other than according to income.
3. Engulf and devour the following:
   a. It's a mistake to have children. They are expensive, difficult to train, and often end up ungrateful for parental efforts.
   b. Since no one can predict how the economy will be in ten years, one is better off spending money on desired items than saving it.
4. Think up a strongest case against the following:
   a. People want only what they cannot have.
   b. Laughter is the best medicine.

5. Make up an argument in favor of dogmatism, then see if you can engulf and devour it. Do the same for relativism and progressivism.

READINGS

1. The best arguments are those which give a counterargument and then show how the case being argued is better. Two examples follow. In each, pick out the argument and its opposing view.

Unhappily, biography has lately been overtaken by a school that has abandoned the selective [aspects of a person's life] in favor of the all-inclusive.... We are presented with the subject's life reconstructed day by day from birth to death, including every new dress or pair of pants, every juvenile poem, every journey, every letter, every loan, every accepted or rejected invitation, every telephone message, every drink at every bar.... I think this development is part of the anti-excellence spirit of our time that insists on the equality of everything and is thus reduced to the theory that all facts are of equal value and that the biographer or historian should not presume to exercise judgment. To that I can only say, if he cannot exercise judgment, he should not be in the business. A portraitist does not achieve a likeness by giving sleeve buttons and shoelaces equal value to mouth and eyes.[2]

Having grasped both arguments, do you agree with the author? One way to discovering whether you agree would be to imagine that there exist two biographies about someone whom you greatly admire: One presents every known fact—"every drink at every bar"—about that person; the other biography tells only about the major events in that person's life along with what the biographer has decided are interesting details. Which would you prefer to read and why?

2. The following are an argument and counterargument on the merits of an artist's career by Dame Janet Baker, a famous opera singer. Can you tell when the counterargument begins? Is her conclusion the same in both arguments? Notice that she is careful to define her major term.

If someone asked if my career has been "worth it," in other words worth the sacrifices made by me and members of my family, worth the separations, the agony of performing, of trying to keep perfectly fit, the undying battle against nerves, the strains and pitfalls of being a public figure, my honest answer would have to be "No."

This sounds a terrible comment to make on a career which, in terms of the world, has been a highly successful one. I have done everything any singer could dream of, yet the moments when the musical rewards have equalled the price one has to pay for them have been few.

But if someone were to ask me how I would choose to be born in order to learn about life, I would unquestionably reply, "As an artist." If it is, as many people suggest, a rather special privilege to be born one, the privilege lies in the opportunities such an existence provides for the individual to learn about himself; in the questions artistic life forces one to ask and try to answer; in the struggle to come to terms with performing and everything implied by an act of heroism, which demands the baring of the soul before strangers, and public judgment of this act; in the choices to be made as a result of loving something more than oneself and serving that something with the greatest integrity one is capable of. Yes, in these terms, my career *has* been "worth it," a thousand times over.[3]

3. Social historian Norbert Elias gives a counterargument to the normal accounts one might give for eating with a fork:

What is the real use of the fork? It serves to lift food that has been cut up to the mouth. Why do we need a fork for this? Why do we not use our fingers? Because it is "cannibal," as . . . the author of *The Habits of Good Society* said in 1859. Why is it "cannibal" to eat with one's fingers? That is not a question; it is self-evidently cannibal, barbaric, uncivilized, or whatever else it is called.

But that is precisely the question. Why is it more civilized to eat with a fork?

"Because it is unhygienic to eat with one's fingers." That sounds convincing. To our sensibility it is unhygienic if different people put their fingers into the same dish, because there is a danger of contracting disease through contact with others. Each of us seems to fear that the others are diseased.

But this explanation is not entirely satisfactory. Nowadays we do not eat from common dishes. Everyone puts food into his mouth from his own plate. To pick it up from one's own plate with one's fingers cannot be more "unhygienic" than to put cake, bread, chocolate, or anything else into one's mouth with one's own fingers.

So why does one really need a fork? Why is it "barbaric" and "uncivilized" to put food into one's mouth by hand from one's own plate? Because it is distasteful to dirty one's fingers, or at least to be seen in society with dirty fingers. The suppression of eating by hand from one's own plate has very little to do with the danger of illness, the so-called "rational" explanation. In observing our feelings toward the fork ritual, we can see with particular clarity that the first authority in our decision between "civilized" and "uncivilized" behavior at table is our feeling of distaste.[4]

NOTES

[1]"Why Holland's South Moluccans Aren't Hijacking Trains Any More," *Wall Street Journal* (New York), May 24, 1984.

[2]Barbara W. Tuchman, *Practicing History* (New York: Alfred A. Knopf, 1981), p. 89.

[3]Janet Baker, *Full Circle* (London: Julia MacRae Publishers, a division of Franklin Watts, 1982), pp. 52–53.

[4]Norbert Elias, *The History of Manners, The Civilizing Process* (New York: Pantheon Books, a division of Random House, Inc., 1978), 1, pp. 126–27.

CHAPTER FOUR

EVIDENCE
An Overview

When challenging someone's argument, we often ask, "What's your evidence?" We're asking whether there are any facts that might persuade us to change our minds. These facts (factual claims) or evidence support the conclusion. Evidence can be either the same as the reason or supportive of a reason. Back to our argument structure for a bit, let's see examples of both uses of the term "evidence."

EVIDENCE AS THE REASON

A piece of evidence can be the reason that a person comes to a conclusion, as in this example:

> **The evidence** Mr. Holmes **offered in his argument** that the heir died **is that** Holmes saw the man's body in the basement (fig. 4.1).

EVIDENCE AS SUPPORTING THE REASON

In other arguments, evidence, rather than being the main reason, *supports* the reason in coming to some conclusion. Evidence usually refers to some-

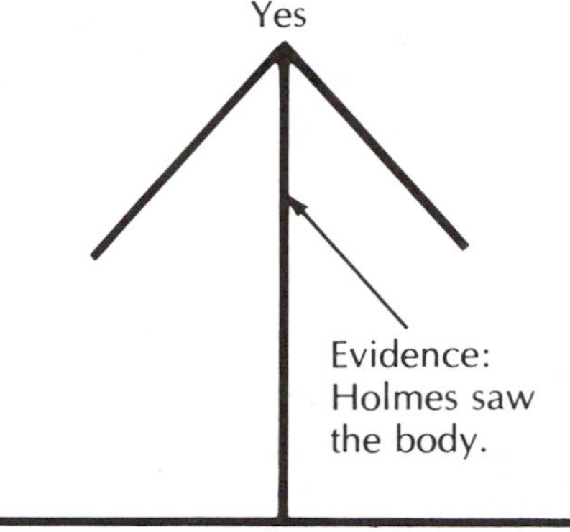

Figure 4.1. Evidence as the reason

thing *seen,* but evidence often refers to a collection of identical things which have been seen or heard, called data.

"Statistical evidence" usually refers to the totaling of similar things or instances. In some arguments the evidence can support a reason or reasons that in turn support the conclusion. For instance:

> The geologist **concluded that** that we will enter another ice age within one hundred years. Her **reasons are that** ice ages have occurred in recent geologic history every ten thousand years and that we are just a few years shy of the beginning of such an interval. She **produced** fossils **as the evidence** dating such climatic change over six ten-thousand-year cycles (see fig. 4.2).

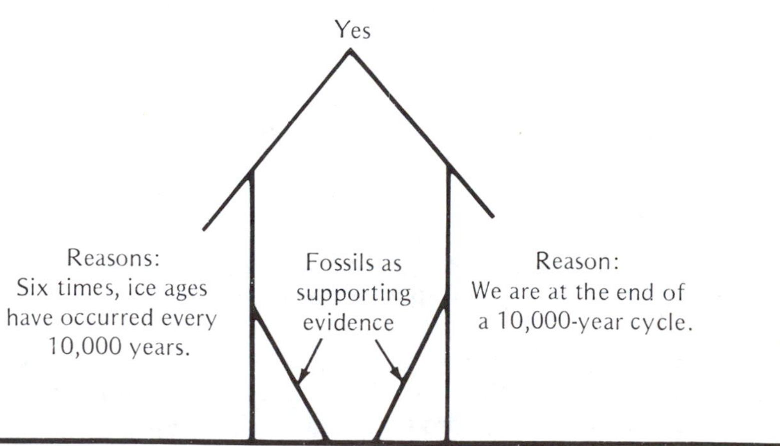

Figure 4.2

You can see from these two examples that the English language isn't precise about the distinction between evidence as reason and evidence in support of a reason. The American Heritage Dictionary defines evidence as "the data on which a judgment or conclusion may be based."[1] It doesn't matter to the *structure* of an argument whether its author decides to call her supporting facts reasons or evidence. It will certainly aid in *clarity*, though, if an author who has a reason and data which support it calls the factual data "evidence."

As you read an argument containing evidentiary claims, ask yourself how the pieces of evidence fit into that argument. Sometimes an author leaves it unclear whether evidence is meant to support a reason or is supposed to stand on its own as a reason. In that case, your job is to realize that the argument could be interpreted either way. In most cases it doesn't make much difference to the argument. What *does* make a difference, however, is failure to pick up on an author's reason, mistakenly taking some evidence for the entire reasoning of an author (e.g., stating that the presence of fossil evidence is the geologist's *sole* reason for concluding that we will enter another ice age).

The ability to skillfully evaluate evidence is crucial to good decision making about arguments. Yet the subject is vast. First, the kind of evidence available varies according to the subject matter. Second, there is more information on more subjects than ever before.

In the teeth of this maze of subjects and evidence, what can we poor critical thinkers do? The following is meant as a useful sketch.

THE KIND OF EVIDENCE DEPENDS ON THE KIND OF ISSUE

Argumentation exists in all academic disciplines. All subject areas make an appeal to evidence in the course of their arguments, but the *kind* of evidence available to any given discipline varies.

Evidence in Science

When we hear arguments that have to do with the nature of the physical world, the evidence will be the result of direct, hands-on experimentation.

For instance, two thousand years ago Greek philosophers speculated upon the argument that the universe is made up of elementary particles (atoms). Other thinkers opposed this notion, with equally strong arguments. No experimental method was yet devised to deal with this and other questions about the physical world. With the advent of the scientific method and its consistent application throughout the past century, however, we have amassed experimental evidence to support the notion of the atomic theory.*

Notice that scientists don't refer to atomic *facts*. A theory is a complex *argument*. Scientific method maintains the balance of "maybe not" by keeping the atomic argument (and all others) open to challenge, despite very strong evidence in its favor. Scientists search for facts but view them as factual claims. So evidence in science hews to the ideal of experimental method.

Examples of scientific questions What is the physical basis of heredity? (Notice that this question does not involve the value judgment whether the theory of DNA or any other theories of heredity are good or bad.) What causes cancer?

Evidence in Philosophy

There are many other questions philosophers, ancient and modern, ponder, such as, "What is the most just society possible?" This question is still of intense interest to philosophers.[2] But unlike questions about the physical world, this one cannot be submitted to hands-on experimentation. What's there to experiment *on*? We are not involved here in a search for what *is* (facts) but in a search for what *should be* (values).

For this reason, the nature of evidence in philosophical argumentation is different from that in science. Philosophers try to explore by argumentation all aspects of values questions. The first task is to explore all the avenues intellectually. Each avenue could eventually evolve into an argument (theory).

One major tack taken by philosophers is to seek a general principle, then think about whether there are cases (evidence) which support that principle. If someone comes up with a counterexample (evidence contrary to the philosopher's position), then the philosopher must revise the principle to take that counterexample into account.

You've seen philosophical arguments twice, once with the Peter Singer argument for equal treatment of animals, and once with the argument about torture. Review each of these arguments for its general principle and significant supporting cases.

This general principle–significant cases technique is used in science too, but there one can always refer back to the hands-on evidence in a way that is not available for questions of value. With questions of value, the ultimate appeal for acceptance of the principle and cases offered is to the audience's reason and experience.

*For further discussion of scientific and philosophical method, see chapter 12.

Evidence in philosophical argumentation is often an appeal to cases offered in support of a principle.

Examples of values questions How should you allocate money for medical research? (Say you run a government agency that allocates money for medical research. There is a painful, devastating disease striking a few thousand people a year. There is another less devastating but more widespread disease. You want to allocate funds for research on both diseases. The amounts that are known about these diseases are about equal. The tasks of trying to eradicate the diseases are equally difficult. How do you put a dollar equivalent on this problem?) If there is a conflict between telling the truth and maintaining social harmony, which should a society value more highly? What kinds of cases can be brought forward as evidence for either position?

Evidence Gathered After the Event

Social, behavioral, and medical scientists can run some experiments on humans. They might look at the metabolism of a new drug in human subjects or use people in learning experiments. But if an experiment has even a chance of being detrimental to a person, the research would be unethical. For example, imagine someone's abusing children to see if they become violent adults. Experiments of this sort would be immoral, only the stuff of horror movies. So in these areas researchers have to use a modified scientific method in the form of statistics-gathering and case studies after the fact. This approach has enhanced our understanding of correlations, but unlike strict scientific method, it can't fully explain how these correlations work.

Here's an example of evidence gathered after the event. Some sports medicine researchers wanted to investigate whether people who exercise vigorously have less risk of dying suddenly of a heart attack. Rather than using hands-on experimentation, keeping people in a laboratory under controlled conditions and *inducing* heart attacks, the researchers chose a humane route. They looked at the records of 1,250 men in Seattle who had died of heart attacks during a fourteen-month period. Thus, the researchers studied these heart attacks after they had happened.

The researchers then eliminated any records from their study that might confuse the evidence. For instance, they eliminated records of people with a history of heart trouble. After all, anyone born with heart disease who does not exercise much and who dies early is as likely to have died of the heart disease as of a lack of exercise.

The researchers found that sedentary men (defined as those who devoted less than twenty minutes per week to vigorous exercise) have almost three times the chance of dying suddenly from a heart attack as do men who exercise vigorously and regularly for more than two and a half hours per week.

This fine study gives good evidence that there is a connection between exercise and cardiovascular health. But we still don't know how this connection works, so we can't manipulate the connection in any way. For all we know, the vigorous exercisers might be doing something else along with the exercise that is actually preventing the heart attacks. Perhaps the sedentary—or the very busy—would like scientists to get at the physical cause of heart attacks and figure out a way for us to bypass exercise altogether, that is, to get the effect of exercise without exercising.

Or consider cigarettes and cancer. There exist any number of after-the-fact case studies linking cigarette smoking and cancer, but there is no way to find out by case studies how cigarette smoke actually changes a normal cell into a cancer cell. That is, there's no way to study the *mechanism* between the two variables, smoking and lung cancer. The case study can show you very strong correlation, which would be very good evidence for the connection, but it doesn't give you any information about mechanism, which is necessary for pinning down the cause-effect relationship between the smoke and cancer. (In fact, laboratory experiments on whole animals and on living cells in culture have provided a theory for the mechanism.)*

Other issues: Whether there is a connection between genetic endowment and criminal behavior; whether there is a correlation between a growing middle class and political revolutions; whether inflation in a country is related to its balance of payments.

HOW DO YOU EVALUATE THE EVIDENCE?

The ability to evaluate evidence skillfully is crucial to good decision making about arguments. Yet the number of issues about which arguments or theories are raised is vast. How to cope?

I think that the best solution is to read widely enough to watch for alternative arguments to issues which interest you. How does the evidence of the argument you favor stack up against the evidence in favor of another view? Even an expert cannot evaluate a theory in her field without considering it in relation to comparable theories. We, too, should "comparison shop" for theories (arguments) which seem to us to provide the best evidence.

Further, since the evidence we learn about is, we hope, offered by experts skilled in experimental method, case studies, or philosophical

*For a further discussion of this example, see chapter 12.

discourse, we must for the most part trust that they made a good-faith effort. But the key is to trust a lot of experts a little bit, reading widely. For expert and novice alike, **critical thinking is the consideration of alternative arguments in light of their evidence.**

GOOD ARGUMENTS DON'T OVERSTEP THEIR EVIDENTIARY LIMITS

A good argument does not trick us into thinking that its evidence is better or of a different type than it is. Here are four rules of thumb:

1. *No matter how dazzling the evidence looks, be skeptical of any claim that an argument has been proven.*

Beware of *any* claim that reads "This evidence *proves* that." If you've looked at scientific journals, the authors of even the most exciting results write "**This evidence suggests that**" or "**This evidence leads us to conclude that,**" but rarely "We have proven that."*

If scientists with their powerful experimental method won't use this term, we should be leery of claims like this one: "They have proven that there are ten personality types." It doesn't matter how much evidence this argument offered; don't accept that it's proven.

On the other hand, if the argument seemed to have some good points, don't reject it entirely.

2. *Shop around for counterarguments.*

Upon reading an argument, think about other arguments or theories (here, of personality). If you are interested and energetic, do more reading on the subject. Expect to find arguments that conflict with the one in question. Weigh the evidence on the side of the "ten types" against the evidence for other theories.

3. *Evaluate the evidence.*

Though we could totally accept or reject this argument, there are many options in between. Depending on how the argument stacks up against other arguments, we could use the following language to evaluate the evidence:

> **The argument presents little (no) evidence that** there are ten personality types.
> The argument **provides some evidence** that . . .
> The author **could marshal (should have marshaled) some evidence that . . .**

*In mathematics, "proof" (of theorems) is a good term.

> The argument **provides good evidence that** ten distinct personality types exist.
> These data **constitute strong evidence that . . .**

4. *Evaluate the argument for how well it assesses its evidence.*

Arguments that accurately assess their evidence usually contain evidence that was conscientiously and skillfully acquired. The "ten personality theories" argument would be a good argument if it dropped the "proof" claim, clearly described its basic structure while defining its major terms, included some good counterarguments, and honestly (even humbly) assessed itself as, say, quite speculative at the moment.

> My theory that there are ten personality types fits a number of situations that I and others have observed. **It is, however, quite speculative at the moment.**

Of course, arguments with strong evidence are entitled to indicate as much.

SUMMARY

Evidence exists in all subject areas. Evidence is material in support of arguments (theories).

The kind of evidence that it is possible to produce depends on the type of argument:

> For a theory about the material world, expect the strongest type of evidence, based on scientific method.
> For a theory about the behavior of human beings, whether as individuals or in social groups, normally expect evidence after the fact in the form of good case studies.
> For a theory about what should be, expect evidence in the form of an appeal to strongest cases.

There are four rules of thumb (for writers and critics):

1. Discount any claim "proving that." Keep every argument open to modification.
2. Shop around for counterarguments and alternative arguments.
3. Entertain options, ranging from no evidence to little evidence to some evidence to good evidence and, finally, to strong evidence.
4. Favorably evaluate arguments that carefully evaluate their evidence.

EXERCISES

1. What kind of evidence would you expect in the following arguments?
   a. An argument that people who eat a special diet will have less chance of getting cancer.
   b. An argument that God exists.
   c. An argument that human cells secrete some substance under certain conditions.
   d. An argument that stealing is unethical.
   e. An argument that owning a pet tends to lower one's blood pressure.

   Answers (a) evidence after the fact; (b) philosophical evidence (a general principle, for instance that the universe is orderly; (c) direct scientific experimentation; (d) philosophical evidence; (e) evidence after the fact
2. Underline the language in the following argument that you believe indicates that it does (or does not) admit its limits.

   It's an obvious fact that living in the suburbs is better than city life. Everyone knows that cities are far more polluted and dangerous. And of course, people don't even know their neighbors. On the other hand, suburbs are peaceful havens from the workaday world.

READING

The following article mentions all three types of evidence. Find the references to each type of evidence, comparing the language used to depict direct experimentation, after-the-fact evidence, and values questions.

Predictive Probes

by Jerry E. Bishop

Several years ago, Nancy Wexler's mother died of Huntington's disease, a hereditary and always-fatal affliction that strikes in midlife. Since then, Ms. Wexler, the 38-year-old president of the Hereditary Diseases Foundation in Santa Monica, Calif., has lived with the uncertainty of whether she, too, inherited the deadly gene.

That uncertainty may soon be resolved. A few months ago, scientists announced they were on the verge of completing a new test to detect the gene for Huntington's disease (formerly called Huntington's chorea). But deciding whether to submit herself to the test is an anguishing choice for Ms. Wexler. "If I came out lucky, taking the test would be terrific, of course," she says. "But if I came out unlucky, well . . . . "

Her dilemma is an extreme example of the kind thousands of Americans will face in the not-too-distant future as scientists learn how to pinpoint genes that cause or predispose a person to a future illness.

The test to detect the Huntington's-disease gene should be ready within one to two years. Researchers already have detected some of the genes that can lead to premature heart attacks and, in the near future, hope to spot those that could predispose a person to breast or colon cancer. Eventually, scientists believe they will be able to detect genes leading to diabetes, depression, schizophrenia and the premature senility called Alzheimer's disease.

"Extraordinary Power"

"This new technology has an extraordinary power to predict any disease where there is any kind of genetic influence," Ms. Wexler says. "Instead of looking in a crystal ball to see your future, you'll look in your genes."

Doctors long have been able to crudely predict a person's future illness. By studying disease patterns, for example, they can say that heavy cigarette smokers have 10 times the risk of developing lung cancer as nonsmokers and that middle-aged men with high blood cholesterol levels have higher-than-normal risk of heart attacks. Geneticists also look at family medical pedigrees to determine the chances of children inheriting any of the 3,000 known genetic disorders.

But such predictions are similar to casino odds. Doctors can't predict which smokers will actually develop lung cancer, which individual will have a premature heart attack or which child actually inherited a defective gene.

Genetic probes, however, will change predictive medicine. The probes are synthetic versions of genes that cause disease. Tossed into a test tube with a small sample of a person's own genetic material—his DNA—the probes cling to and identify their natural counterparts.

"Raft of Questions"

Proponents of predictive medicine cite its potentially tremendous benefit in that it will allow, in some instances, people to take preventive measures to ward off certain illnesses. "But it also raises a raft of questions on almost every level—social, psychological, personal, legal and ethical," says Ms. Wexler, a psychologist who has specialized in the problems of victims of genetic diseases. Such problems range from how and when to tell a seemingly healthy person he or she has a gene for a possibly fatal disease to whether employers, insurance companies, or even the government should know a person carries such a gene.

Nowhere are the social and ethical questions surrounding genetic probes more apparent than in the case of Huntington's disease.

Although the disease is caused by inheritance of a mutant gene, the symptoms usually don't show up until between ages 30 and 50. The disease is characterized by slow but steady mental deterioration that begins with moodiness and ends fatally with severe mental illness. One tragedy is that carriers of the fatal gene often don't know their condition before having children of their own. Children whose parents are known carriers grow up haunted by the 50% probability that they, too, carry the gene.

Late last year, however, a team of scientists from several institutions reported making a breakthrough that will lead to a test for the Huntington's-disease gene. With the aid of experimental genetic probes, James F. Gusella, a doctor at Massachusetts General Hospital, and his colleagues studied the genes of 135 members of a large family in Venezuela that is plagued by Huntington's disease. While the team didn't find the gene itself, they did discover an unusual genetic variation that seems to accompany the mysterious gene when it is passed along. Hence, it might serve as a "marker" for the Huntington disease gene.

Preparing for Problems

Dr. Gusella and Integrated Genetics Inc., a small biotechnology company he works with, are sifting through genes of Huntington's-disease families looking for a second genetic marker, which would make the test more than 99% accurate. They then must confirm the mutant gene as the only cause of Huntington's disease, meaning the test probably won't be available for a year or two.

Researchers, however, already are preparing for problems the test will create. At Indiana University, medical geneticists since 1979 have located and compiled medical and genetic information on 34,000 people from Huntington's-disease families, including 5,000 who are still alive. Once the test is perfected, each of those 5,000 persons at risk must decide whether to take it.

"Roughly half of them say they want to know, and the other half say they don't want to know," says Joe E. Christian, a physician and chairman of the medical-genetics department at Indiana. "Many people said, 'Don't take away my last hope' by telling them that they definitely have the gene."

Whether the spouse or potential spouse should be told is a matter to be addressed in a program planned by Huntington's-disease centers at Massachusetts General Hospital and Johns Hopkins University, Dr. Gusella says. "Nothing has been settled yet, but the consensus seems to be that the person being tested gets the information and it will be up to him whether anyone else should be told." In any case, he adds, "there will have to be a maximum of pre-test counseling and post-test support."

Another issue is whether employers or insurance companies paying for the test are entitled to know the results. Health-insurance data go into a central computer and are available to all insurance companies. As it is, says Ms. Wexler of the Hereditary Disease Foundation, persons at risk of Huntington's disease can buy life insurance from only a few companies and then only at almost prohibitive rates.

Such problems won't be unique to Huntington's disease much longer. Probes for other diseases are certain to raise similar questions. "An executive might be passed up for promotion if it became known that he carried the gene for familial hypercolesterolemia (inherited high cholesterol) with its high risk of premature heart attacks," says Arno Motulsky, a doctor and a geneticist at the University of Washington. "Could one blame an industrial company for such action? Do individuals who know they carry such a gene have the right to withhold such information from employers?"

Despite those thorny questions, the geneticists are hard at work. Among their targets are the genes that cause atherosclerosis, the clogging of the arteries with fatty deposits. Atherosclerosis is a slow, silent disease that can lead to heart attacks in the adult years. And recently it has become clear that the rapidity with which arteries clog is determined by defects or variations in any of at least eight genes that control the way the body uses and disposes of fats. Genetic probes will be able to detect these genetic defects and variations long before a heart attack develops.

An early demonstration of that new predictive power already is under way involving an inherited disorder called familial dysbetalipoproteinemia. Victims of the disorder, which is uncommon but not necessarily rare, have such high amounts of cholesterol and other fats in their circulation that the blood serum is actually cloudy. The consequences begin to show up in early adulthood in men and later in women when the arteries in the limbs and heart become severely clogged. Unless treated, the victims suffer heart attacks in their 20s or 30s.

Scientists now know that at least 95% of people suffering this rapid artery-clogging have two copies of a gene called the apo E-2 gene, having inherited one copy from each parent. Recently, Jan Breslow, a doctor at Rockefeller University, and some collaborators at Harvard University, where Dr. Breslow worked before joining Rockefeller, developed genetic probes that detect both normal and mutant forms of the gene. The probes now can be used to determine whether the new-found mutant genes are responsible for the disease.

Genetic probes will allow doctors to detect such atherosclerosis genes at birth by taking umbilical cord blood and looking for lesions at the DNA level, Dr. Breslow says. If the infant is found to have genes that predispose him or her to an early heart attack, "we can begin to practice true prevention," he says. Cancer researchers have similar hopes for genetic probes. Scientists now are finding evidence supporting a theory proposed a few years ago by Alfred G. Knudsen, a doctor at Philadelphia's Fox Chase Cancer Center. While studying a type of childhood eye cancer known to be inherited, he speculated it took two "hits," or events, for the eye cancer to occur. The first hit would be the inheritance of a gene (or the absence of a gene, as it actually turned out) that had the potential of causing cancer. Then a second hit had to occur before the gene (or lack of a gene) turned a cell malignant and led to a tumor. The hypothesis is holding up in the case of certain childhood cancers, Dr. Knudsen says, adding, "It's a good bet that at least some adult cancers are caused by the same mechanism."

Researchers note, for example, that daughters of breast-cancer patients have a 10% higher risk of developing breast cancer than other women. Thus, it seems that a predisposition to breast cancer can be inherited. But only a small portion of such daughters develop breast cancer. Dr. Knudsen's two-hit hypothesis would explain that situation. While perhaps a fourth of all women whose mothers or grandmothers had breast cancer carry a cancer-prone gene—the first hit—only a small portion actually suffer the still unidentified second hit that leads to malignancy.

If Dr. Knudsen's hypothesis is true, then genetic probes would tell a woman if she inherited the first-hit gene. Those who did would be forewarned to have frequent breast examinations to catch the tumor in its early, curable stage.

As with breast cancer and other physical ailments, there is evidence that certain behavioral illnesses can be inherited. For example, studies indicate that a tendency to depression and manic depression can run in families. And now there is a growing suspicion that Alzheimer's disease, the senility and loss of memory that usually strikes its victims in their late 50s or early 60s, has a genetic aspect.

If that suspicion is borne out, and if probes can uncover the predisposing genes early, the question of how such probes should be used becomes complex. One question: Could persons carrying such genes be banned from managerial or executive positions or even high political offices where their decisions affect large numbers of people?

To the University of Washington's Dr. Motulsky, the notion of genetic screening isn't that farfetched. "As public bodies assume a more direct role in the health system in many countries," he said, "confidentiality may become eroded and genetic information may be used by social and health planners to assign individuals their niche in society."[3]

NOTES

[1]*The American Heritage Dictionary* (Boston: American Heritage Publishing Co., Inc., and Houghton Mifflin Company, 1981), s.v. "evidence."

[2]See John Rawls, *A Theory of Justice* (Cambridge, Mass.: Harvard University Press, 1971); Robert Nozick, *Anarchy, State and Utopia* (New York: Basic Books, 1974); Michael Walzer, *Spheres of Justice* (New York: Basic Books, 1983).

[3]*Wall Street Journal* (New York), September 12, 1984, p. 1, col. 1.

CHAPTER FIVE

DECIDING TO ACCEPT AN ARGUMENT

Warranted Inference

This chapter links several of the ideas you have learned in foregoing chapters.

The framework of an argument is an issue being brought to some conclusion with the support of reasons. Also bear in mind that arguments vary in the strength of their structures. Some reasons are strongly supportive of their conclusions; others aren't. Another way of saying this is that some inferences (conclusions) are warranted, or "deserved," because of the strength of their reasons or evidence; other inferences are not warranted. To pursue the house analogy, some posts strongly support their roofs, while other roofs cave in. The inference is thus the roof *and* the spot where the posts join the roof.

TWO REQUIREMENTS FOR WARRANTED INFERENCE

Two factors are necessary for an inference to be warranted, and thus worthy of your acceptance: (1) the reasons must be *true,* and (2) the conclusion must *follow* from the reasons. We will look at each of these factors in turn.

The Reasons Must Be True

For the conclusion, and therefore the argument, to be warranted, the reason or reasons supporting it must be true. If the reasons are false, the argument collapses.

Unfortunately, we can't literally see arguments "collapse," although they are frequently described as doing so. To take an example from the history of medicine:

> The nineteenth-century view of tuberculosis was that it was strictly psychosomatic. It was thought that people who were too artistic or angelic for this world were its primary victims. This theory collapsed with the discovery of the tubercle bacillus.

According to this author, on the issue whether tuberculosis is a psychosomatic disease, the nineteenth-century view was in the affirmative, the reason (evidence) being that extremely artistic or angelic people had a greater tendency to contract it. This inference is not warranted in light of current evidence. Instead, our reason for believing that people contract tuberculosis is that certain bacteria called tubercle bacilli have infected their lungs. The twentieth-century layman's view of the cause of tuberculosis is physical.

This is "the *layman's* view," the ordinary argument that we make in thinking about the cause of tuberculosis. But as you know from chapter 4, this argument is based on more complicated evidence and assumes the provisional acceptance of that evidence until better comes along.

Although the layman's argument is as short as the nineteenth-century view, it is at the moment a lot better supported by evidence. Since it is well supported, its inference is, for the time being, *warranted*. By the same token, there is no evidence to support the notion that angelic or artistic people are more prone to tuberculosis, and so that inference is not warranted unless further evidence comes along.

The language of truth assessment is illustrated in the following examples:

> Because it is **not the case that** more artistic people die of tuberculosis, the author's **conclusion is not warranted.**
>
> **It is not true that . . . . Therefore . . .** the author's **conclusion is not justified** by these reasons.
>
> The author claims that most people are dissatisfied with their jobs. **This, in fact, is not the case.**
>
> **It is not true that** job dissatisfaction is rampant.

The Conclusion Must Follow from the Reasons

Not only must the reason or reasons be true, but they must directly lead to that conclusion. Other, related conclusions require their own reasons.

It can be easy to jump the track. For instance, once aware that tuberculosis is a well-understood and easily cured disease, you might be tempted to draw the additional inference that TB is not a health problem in the United States. That *might* be the case, but it doesn't directly follow from the argument of what the cause of tuberculosis is. And unfortunately, despite good understanding of the disease and readily available medication, an estimated 23,500 people in the United States alone developed TB in 1983, and more people died from it than from all other specific communicable diseases combined.[1] So just because the cause and cure of TB are known, *it does not follow* that tuberculosis is no health problem.

Nor is it proper to infer from known evidence about the tubercle bacillus that any lung disease is understood or curable. For example, there is a lung ailment, sarcoid, which causes a TB-like inflammation, but for which the infectious agent is not known. It does not follow that because some diseases are understood, all diseases, including sarcoid, must be understood. Therefore, as you read or hear an argument, be sure to ask yourself, "Does this conclusion really follow from these reasons?"

TWO TYPES OF INFERENCE

In one type of inference, called *deduction,* the conclusion should *necessarily* follow; in the other, *induction,* the conclusion should *likely* follow. "Should" is used here because both induction and deduction can misfire as well as be sound, as you will see.

Deduction

We often perform the mental operation of drawing a more particular conclusion out of an *all*-encompassing reason.

For instance:

All-encompassing reason: *All* the people in this class are friendly.
Particular conclusion: Therefore, the person sitting next to me in this class must be friendly.

The conclusion about a particular classmate was *deduced* from the general idea that all the people in the class are friendly.

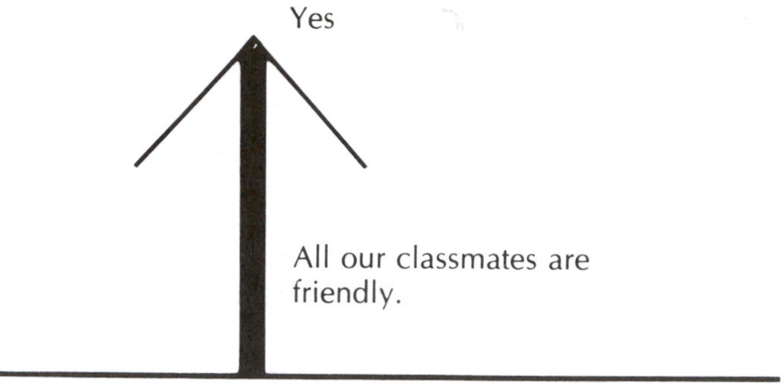

Issue: Whether our classmate Frenelda is friendly.

Figure 5.1

Figure 5.1 shows by a much thicker wall beam that the reason is more general—*all* classmates—than the conclusion, which involves one particular classmate. Let's call her Frenelda.

Take a moment to realize that if the reason is true, then the conclusion has to be true too. If all our classmates are friendly and Frenelda is a classmate, she *has to be friendly,* given the way the argument is set up. This is really the essence of a valid deduction: The conclusion is *necessarily* the case if the reason is true. That particular instance of Frenelda as friendly is already a part of the notion that everyone in the class is friendly. The conclusion is actually contained inside the reason. That is why the conclusion "roof" is planted firmly on top of the reason.

Now comes a surprise. Even if it is *not true* that all our classmates are friendly, this deduction is technically valid. That is because the logic still follows, that is, *supposing that* all our classmates are friendly, classmate Frenelda has to be friendly by logical necessity. When the reasons of a valid deduction are not true, that deduction is *unsound,* and the inference is not warranted. The ideal, of course, is to strive for true reasons and a valid deductive (all-encompassing) form.

There are an infinite number of things one can fit into this deductive scheme. The key is in the use of "all," "every," and "only" as adjectives in front of the major reason in an argument. For example, granting the notion that all ripe oranges taste good, you would have to conclude that any ripe oranges you eat this year will taste good. You start with the inclusive idea (any ripe oranges) and fit a smaller group (the ripe oranges you will eat this year) inside of it. Of course, the "smaller" group can be quite large. For instance, from the notion that all oranges taste good, I can deduce that all the ripe oranges consumed by Americans over the past fifty years tasted good. That is a lot of oranges.

Another common deductive mode is to be *all-exclusive.*
For instance:

Because no person is a louse and Francie is a person, Francie is not a louse (at least not in the literal sense).

Again, the deduction is valid because the two categories, person and louse, are claimed to be totally excluded from each other.

Here is a famous deduction, in a form called a syllogism:

All men are mortal (first reason, also called a *premise*).
Socrates is a man (second reason, or premise).
Therefore, Socrates is mortal (conclusion).

This form of writing is seldom found in ordinary prose. It does serve, however, to lay bare the logical bones of an argument.

The previous two examples reflect the two commonest valid deductive forms:

All X are Y.
Z is an X (or all Z are X; or some Z are X).
Therefore, Z is a Y.*
No X are Y.
Z is an X (or Z is a Y).
Therefore, Z is not a Y. (Therefore, Z is not an X.)

You might want to amuse yourself by concocting deductions to fit these patterns. Remember,

In a valid deduction, the conclusion *inevitably follows* from an all-encompassing reason or reasons.

Deductions can be valid (logical) without their reasons or conclusions being true.

A deduction must be valid and true for its conclusion (inference) to be warranted.

Induction

Induction is more cautious than deduction. Many times it would bend the truth to make a reason all-encompassing, for instance to claim

*Notice that the following deductive form is invalid:

All X are Y.	All men are mortal
Z is Y.	Fido is mortal.
Therefore, Z is an X.	Therefore, Fido is a man.

that *all* the people in the South have southern accents. But it is true to claim that *most* people in the South have southern accents. So the warranted inference can be made that the next person encountered on the street in New Orleans is *likely* to have a southern accent. Because "likely" is used, even if the next person met doesn't have a southern accent the inference is still good. The only way in which the inference will fall apart is that "Most people in the South have southern accents" is not true (e.g., if there have been so many people from other parts of the United States or abroad moving to the South).

This "most" is a very useful tool. Think of the instances in which you use inductive reasoning daily, as well as receive information based on inductions made by the community of thinkers:

> Most people who don't wear seat belts and get in accidents suffer greater injuries than those people who wear seat belts. So if you wear a seat belt you are likely to be less severely injured in an accident.
>
> Most of the time when bond prices fall, stocks rise. Since today bond prices are falling, the chances are good that stock prices are rising.
>
> Most people are mortal. Socrates is a person. Therefore Socrates is probably mortal.

In another form of induction you can start with fewer than "most." A number of similar particular instances come to mind, and from them you arrive at a more general conclusion. One can use any example, but let's take oranges. You notice that the orange you're eating is delicious. That reminds you of one you ate last week, and as you remember other particular orange-eating experiences, you find yourself happily anticipating that future oranges you eat this year should taste good. You have thus *moved from a number of particulars to a generalization,* making an inductive leap: On the basis of these past particular oranges, the next oranges are *likely* to taste as good.

Because of their more tentative, "likely" nature, inductions are entitled to larger conclusions than their reasons. Take the example of the class again. Rather than starting out with the reason that all the people in the class are friendly, you might be wondering about that very point. So you speak to your neighbors on either side of you and to the person sitting in front and behind you. On the basis of friendly discussions with several neighbors, you come to the conclusion that most of the people in this class seem friendly (see fig. 5.2).

Notice that the roof is floating just above the posts. This is meant to symbolize that moving from particulars to a generalization involves a leap, called the "inductive leap." The same leap is, of course, true in any

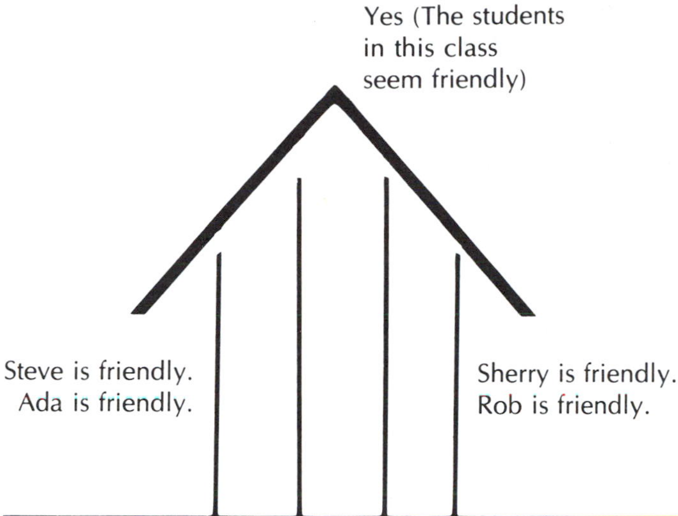

Figure 5.2

case of "most." Assume here that there are more than four students in this class and that these four are a fraction of the total, say twenty. Here you have actually "polled," or "tested," four particulars to leap to the conclusion about most. Notice how crucial that "most" is; it's hard enough to leap from "some" to "most"; given this small sample, one may not conclude that all the students are likeable.

Deduction and Induction

The mind can rapidly make deductions and inductive leaps, all within a few seconds. Most intellectual endeavor is a complicated combination of deductive and nondeductive thought. You may baffle yourself if you think about your present opinion of oranges or anything else, wondering how your mind traveled (all-inclusive general belief, fitting a more particular conclusion? particular oranges to a more general conclusion about them?). Doubtless it has done both, about oranges and countless other issues.

Things Can Go Wrong with Deduction and Induction

Both inductive and deductive arguments can collapse. Here are some quick tests for strength:

For deduction: When an argument gives an all-encompassing reason and a more particular conclusion, ask

1. Is that generalization *true,* as best you can figure? (Can you think of counter-examples to the reason?)
2. Then, accepting the truth of the reasons for the moment, does the conclusion *have to follow*? Or could it be otherwise?

Both items 1 and 2 must obtain for a warranted inference.

For induction: When an argument reasons from "most" or a number of particulars, ask

1. Are the particular cases or the claim of "most" *true,* as far as you know?
2. Are there *enough particular cases* to justify making a generalization?
3. Does the generalization *follow from* those particulars?

Items 1, 2, and 3 are required for a warranted inference.

Under no circumstances go from one instance to all or always. For example,

> I know of a man who wore his seat belt and was in an auto accident but didn't suffer any injuries. Therefore anyone who wears a seat belt and is in an auto accident will not suffer many injuries.

Safe Inductive Leaps

With inductive leaps you want to ask, "Have I got enough individual cases to safely generalize about this matter?" If I like four people in my class, is it a warranted inference (safe generalization) that most of the people in my class are likeable? If the four people I picked as individual cases were the dear friends with whom I enrolled in the class, my generalization is not warranted. If I tried to walk up to four classmates, more or less at random, to speak to them, my chances are better (though not excellent) for assessing the general likeableness of people in the class.

This is common sense. What is not commonsensical, but an impressive feat, is the way statisticians can take a small sampling of people and predict how vast numbers will probably behave, say, in the voting booth. This powerful prediction technique has only developed over the last century.

Statisticians' methods are complex and vary from task to task. Thanks to their efforts, we are provided with daily information from surveys and other collections of data. For reasons discussed in chapter 4, the behavioral sciences are particularly dependent on statistical data.

The key idea behind the success of this method is to make the small sample (the particulars) reflect as accurately as possible the large group under study. So, for example, to successfully predict how an election will turn out, one needs samples of people that represent a cross section of all voters. If the voting public is a certain percentage of low-income people (and it's been found beforehand that income affects voting in a certain way), then the same percentage of low-income people must be in the sample. Of course, because surveying people takes time and money, the fewer the people or events or things needed, the better.

Inductive leaps of this sort, called *predictions,* are based on probability theory, which is a branch of mathematics. Over time and with trial and error, these predictions have been greatly refined.

As critical thinkers reading about the results of some survey or poll, we're in scant position to be able to judge how faithful the polltakers were to these statistical requirements. But assuming reputable and knowledgeable data-gathering, we can still critically evaluate the results of a survey if we know what questions were asked. For instance, if a survey claims that people are not concerned about tropical deforestation, but the kinds of questions asked could lead people to give the answers they did because they didn't *know* about the incidence of tropical deforestation, the conclusion that people don't care is not warranted by the data from the survey.

So the main task in assessing a statistically gathered collection of data is to ask, "Does the generalization *follow from* those particulars?" In other words, were the questions asked which would warrant the inference?

Language for Calling Attention to an Unwarranted Inference

Chapter 13 is devoted entirely to fallacies and problems of inconsistency. For the time being, however, notice the language often used to point to an unwarranted inference:

> It is **not immediately apparent how** the **reason offered** by the author that there is unrest in the Middle East is **relevant to** the **question whether** the United States should spend less money on its space program. Therefore, the author's conclusion that less money should be spent is unwarranted.
>
> Smith's **conclusion** that we should turn the other cheek **is not consistent with** her earlier claim that we should always act to defend our rights. She **must reconcile** these ideas; at present, her inference is not warranted.
>
> X's inference that people should take their grievances to court **is unwarranted, because** it is **inconsistent with** his **reasoning that** people are by nature unfair to one another. If people are so unfair, X has failed to explain why a judge and jury would be any different.

A Flexible Mind

The critical mind has fun constantly sorting things out, trying out new ideas and seeing if particular situations fit. If the particulars don't seem to fit, a new general idea is called for.

People can suffer from two types of inflexibility. Some seem to hate generalizations. As the saying goes, they can't see the forest for the trees. Have you ever met someone who talks *only* about disconnected particulars, say, giving you every nattering detail about some conversation about which you have no interest? If only that person would tie those details to some useful generalization, for example, the way that Americans in their twenties interact with one another or use slang in a certain way, anything that will lift this material into something worth thinking about. Either of these topics might also bore you, but at least you have a chance to get to another topic of more general interest. It is very hard to pull out of the nose dive into a thicket of unrelated details. The world is full of an infinite number of details, and life is short. If you get stuck listening to such a conversation, you might try to find a spot to come in with "Well, that's very interesting. Do you think that the way she swore at him is *characteristic* of the way women speak to men these days?" Asking whether something is characteristic or typical or often done is a quick way to get to a bigger picture.

At the other extreme, some people generalize without letting the breeze of fresh events blow in. There is the pompous type who can speak only in opinionated conclusions and never seems to let some new or unusual occurrence modify his stale deductions. His mind's made up; don't confuse him with factual claims. Particular events need some general notions to make them significant; general ideas need constant testing against particular instances to make sure that they're right.

You could critically evaluate the foregoing argument by using your reason and experience.

WHETHER A CONCLUSION IS WARRANTED

There are many controversial arguments whose conclusions hinge on the truth of some additional claims, the certainty of which is hard to know. Those "linchpin" claims are fascinating to tease out. It's important to realize that the argument will hold (i.e., will be warranted) only if such additional facts are true. Do you remember Agnes's dilemma in chapter 2 about whether she needed to go to the market? Her conclusion hinged on the question whether her brother had already gone. These kinds of arguments have the same structure.

Take, for example, the loose argument that the world will run out of oil. One might take issue, replying, "That inference is warranted only if other energy sources don't supplant oil." Can you think of any other fact or facts which would have to be true to warrant this inference? Or take the controversial question whether the Democratic or Republican political philosophy is better for the country. One might argue that the Democrats' inference that social programs are necessary for economic improvement is warranted only if the private sector cannot or will not provide jobs for anyone who is willing to work hard. One could also argue that the Republicans' inference that there should be a minimum of government interference in private enterprise is warranted only if such minimum interference results in greater benefits for all of society.

Do you agree that these inferences are warranted only if these additional facts must be true? Can you think of other necessary facts in these cases?

DECIDE AND DO WITH BALANCE

Don't infer from the foregoing that you're supposed to keep an eternally suspended judgment about controversial areas that hinge on hard-to-verify facts. Quite the contrary—it is hoped that you will use the techniques described in this book to decide issues and act accordingly. Otherwise, what's the point of learning to think critically?

Base your decision on the available evidence, on your reasoning powers, and on your experience—your personal experience and claims you've heard and read from among the community of thinkers and believe to be reliable.

Just because you decide and then act doesn't mean that you are not still in balance, still open to future arguments as to why you should change your mind and act differently.

CHECK CAREFULLY FOR CONSISTENCY

Most people who carefully review an argument can detect major errors of irrelevance and inconsistency, thereby seeing that the conclusion does not follow from the reasons. When an instructor tactfully points out an inconsistency in a student's paper, that student usually laughs—a healthy response. The point is to get into the habit of careful checking of both one's own work and that of others.

As you read, constantly ask yourself "Does this conclusion really follow from the reason(s) offered? Really?" Asking this question requires a lot more mental effort than passive absorption of the material.

On the assumption that humor, besides being enjoyable, can effectively show inconsistency, let's look at a wacky argument that doesn't obey these rules of consistency and relevance. What's wrong with this picture?

> Money is not everything, but it is better than having one's health. After all, one cannot go into a butcher shop and tell the butcher, "Look at my great suntan, and besides I never catch colds," and expect him to hand over any merchandise.[2]

The issue is whether having money is better than having health. Suggest the reason(s) for the argument. Do you feel foolish suggesting reasons? Whether you can get food for free by proclaiming yourself healthy is not *relevant* to the issue of whether having money is better than having health.

But while it's necessary that the reasons be relevant to warrant a conclusion, relevance alone is not sufficient. Here's an example showing why:

> It's important for people to make sacrifices for one another. One reason is that it's vital for people to do what they want every moment of their lives.

Do you detect any inconsistency? If you don't, reread the example and think about these two ideas, self-sacrifice and doing what one wants. You probably realize that these two ideas are often in opposition. They are therefore relevant to one another, but they are inconsistent and belong in opposing arguments.

In short, a reason that is irrelevant is off the issue entirely; an inconsistent reason is on the issue but does not fit the conclusion. (For a further discussion of consistency, see chapter 13.)

CIRCULAR REASONING

One might call this problem "overconsistency." A person offers the conclusion as the reason for the same conclusion. Children often like to sing, "We're here because we're here because we're here." For instance,

> Money is better than poverty, if only for financial reasons.[3]

Think for a minute. Is the argument relevant and consistent? It is. But since the reasons (financial) are identical with the term "money," there are actually no reasons (you can't hold up your roof with more of the roof). This statement is not a strict argument even though it pretends to be by offering a reason. Such an attempt to support a conclusion by using the conclusion itself as the reason is called circular reasoning.

DISAGREEING WITH GOOD ARGUMENTS

It is entirely possible to see that an argument is strongly supported, its inference(s) warranted, and still disagree with it. You might disagree because you can think of *even stronger* reasons in support of a different conclusion (the engulf and devour of "even granting"). "Stronger reasons" mean reasons that are still consistent with the conclusion, yet more relevant, taking in more factors, and more likely to be true as far as you can figure at the moment. An argument with such reasons is therefore, in your opinion, better supported.

Be wary of instances in which you can see that an argument is strongly supported but disagree with it without being able to strongly support your disagreement. You may be entirely right to disagree, but you should be certain that you have not yet worked out why you disagree, and therefore you don't yet know whether you're right to reject the argument. You know only that it doesn't seem right. You might either file it away under "doesn't seem right, I don't agree, will perhaps take it up later" or think about it right away. In the interest of truth, however, it's not fair to say "I disagree, so the argument must be wrong." That is a whopper of an unwarranted inference.

By the same token, it is entirely possible to agree heartily with the conclusion of an argument and not agree that the reasons are relevant or true or consistent with the conclusion, or even consistent with one another.

SUMMARY

A warranted inference is a conclusion that is deserved because of the strong reasons which support it. Strong reasons are reasons which are true and which directly lead to the conclusion.

There are two types of inference, deduction and induction:

> In deduction, an all-encompassing reason leads to a more particular conclusion. In a warranted deduction, the conclusion inevitably follows from an all-encompassing reason. The reason(s) must be true.
>
> In induction, a reason containing a number of particulars persuades us of a "most likely all" or "most likely this" conclusion. In a warranted inductive leap, there are a sufficient number of particulars which make up the reason. These particulars are true.

Under no circumstances should you reason from one instance to "all" or "always."

EXERCISES

1. Language review
   a. **Just because** she is late for class every day **does not** ____ **the inference that** she is lazy.
   b. **By** ____ that anyone who is beaten as a child will become a child abuser, he **has overstated his case** (i.e., has jumped to a conclusion that is too broad for the reasons given).
   c. He **justified** this ____ **by** an appeal to common sense.
   d. She **supported** her ____ **with** numerous references from the technical literature.
   e. I am **not certain that one can draw the** ____ **that** because the average man makes twice as much money as the average woman, men have deliberately held women back economically.
   f. The author's **claim is** ____ **with** her earlier argument. She has not contradicted herself.
   g. **It is** ____ for any company **to claim** that it can in all cases be an equal opportunity employer as well as an affirmative action employer.
   h. **Although it is true that** more poor than rich people commit crimes, **the** ____ that poverty causes crime is ____.

   Answers (a) warrant; (b) inferring; (c) inference (or conclusion); (d) conclusion (or inference); (e) inference; (f) consistent; (g) inconsistent; (h) inference . . . unwarranted. (Even if you believe that poverty does cause crime and that the inference *is* warranted, the author has set up the sentence with "although" so that the negative intent is clear.)
2. Review the examples in chapter 3 and decide whether each is a deductive or an inductive argument.
3. Catch yourself moving from some all-inclusive generalization to tucking a particular instance inside, or leaping to a generalization of "most" from a number of particular instances. Come up with three examples of each.
4. If some of the legislators in Congress are industrious, does it necessarily follow that all the legislators are industrious?
5. Say you find an '83 Dodge Dart that is for sale at a cheap price. You have a mechanic check the motor out.
   a. Will he be thinking deductively, inductively, or both as he checks the motor for flaws? Why do you think so?
   b. You then consult *Consumer Reports* for the repair record on '82 Dodge Darts. Is the repair record the result of inductive or deductive thinking or both? How?
6. Assume that you knew a man who drank chaparral tea and got over his lumbago.
   a. Would it be a warranted inference that anyone suffering from lumbago can be cured by drinking chaparral tea?
   b. If you administered chaparral tea to 100 lumbago sufferers and 70 got better, would it be a warranted inference that anyone suffering from lumbago can be cured by drinking chaparral tea? Would it be a warranted inference that a person might be cured by drinking chaparral tea?

READINGS

1. Here is a theory to explain accounts reported in many places around the world of the killing of people by casting evil spells. Do you believe that the author's inference is warranted? Can you think of another explanation of this eerie phenomenon?

An individual who is aware that he is the object of sorcery is thoroughly convinced that he is doomed according to the most solemn traditions of his group. His friends and relatives share this certainty. From then on the community withdraws. Standing aloof from the accursed, it treats him not only as though he were already dead but as though he were a source of danger to the entire group. On every occasion and by every action, the [society] suggests death to the unfortunate victim, who no longer hopes to escape what he considers to be his ineluctable fate. Shortly thereafter, sacred rites are held to dispatch him to the realm of shadows [death]. First brutally torn from all of his family and social ties and excluded from all functions and activities through which he experienced self-awareness, then banished by the same forces from the world of the living, the victim yields to the combined effect of intense terror, the sudden total withdrawal of . . . the support of the group, and, finally, to the group's decisive reversal in proclaiming him—once a living man, with rights and obligations—dead and an object of fear, ritual and taboo. Physical integrity [the body] cannot withstand the dissolution of the social personality.[4]

2. What do you think of the following argument by Edward de Bono about humor?

Humor provides an escape from the rigidity of the YES/NO system [of normal logic in which an idea is either right (yes) or wrong (no)] . . . . Humor has its own rules. In humor you are allowed to say things which are obviously wrong or at best unlikely . . . . [Yet an] explanation is funny because it does have a surface plausibility. The explanation has meaning for we can see the crazy logic involved. The ideas do fit together as ideas even though they do not reflect reality.[5]

NOTES

[1]K. Freifeld, "Wasting Away," *Forbes*, July 30, 1984, p. 122.

[2]Woody Allen, *Without Feathers* (New York: Ballantine Books, a division of Random House, Inc., 1983), p. 109.

[3]*Ibid.*

[4]Claude Levi-Strauss, *Structural Anthropology* (New York: Doubleday & Company, 1967), p. 161.

[5]Edward de Bono, *Practical Thinking* (New York: Penguin Books, 1983), p. 138.

CHAPTER SIX

OTHER CONNECTIONS
Assumptions and Implications

One of the most exciting facts about arguments is that they contain parts which are frequently invisible unless sought out. Assumptions lie beneath the argument and constitute the basement of the structure; implications are a weather vane which points above and beyond the structure, pointing to areas outside the argument that the argument will affect (see fig. 6.1).

THE BEST ARGUMENTS EXPOSE THEIR MAJOR ASSUMPTIONS

Each argument has an enormous number of assumptions, for instance that the world exists and that the argument is comprehensible. But these assumptions don't affect our acceptance of an argument (that the world exists doesn't affect my views of a theory that capital punishment is a deterrent to criminals). But there are assumptions beneath arguments for capital punishment (for instance, that criminals are as rational as non-criminals), which would affect my acceptance of a theory of capital punishment. These types of assumptions are the major assumptions of an argument. **A major assumption is a claim, which, if you knew it, would be a significant factor influencing your decision to accept that argument.**

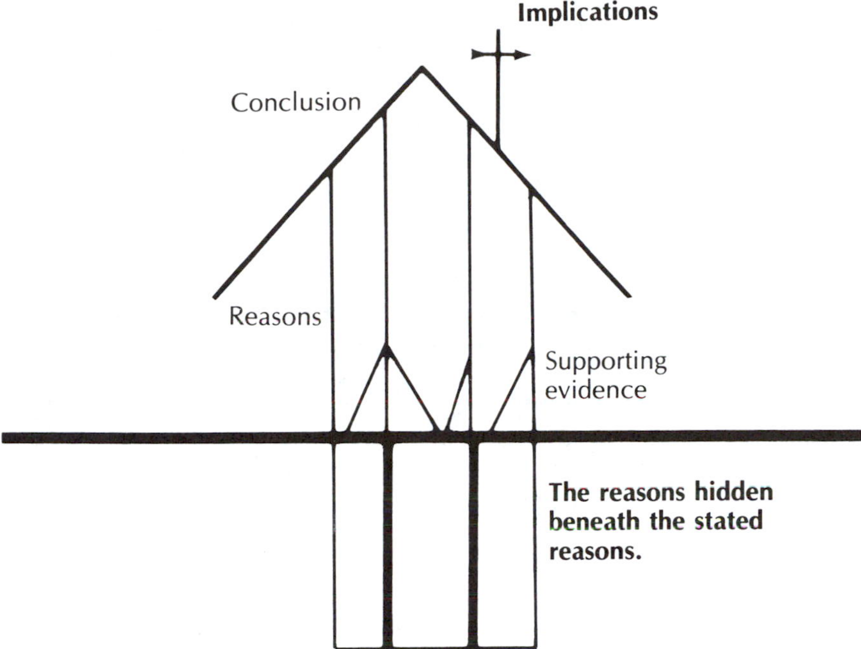

Figure 6.1

If an author is exposing an assumption, it will be with some form of these terms: "assumes," "presupposes," or "presumes." These words should convey the sense of something *beneath the reasons* that is different from them. Here is the language commonly used:

I am **assuming that . . .**
The presupposition here **is that . . .**
The presumption is that . . .
Given the assumption that . . .
The author's claim is **predicated on the assumption that . . .**

MANY ARGUMENTS, HOWEVER, DO NOT DISPLAY THEIR ASSUMPTIONS

Locating and bringing up hidden assumptions for scrutiny is enlightening. But notice the wording: "bringing up." *If "assumes," "presupposes," or "presumes" isn't used somehow in a statement, then the statement is probably not an assumption.* This cannot be stressed enough. Don't light on some hapless reason sitting innocently in the argument and label it the assumption.

There are two good ways to flush hidden assumptions from below. One is to think of a counterargument; the other is to seek a pivotal term.

Think of a counterargument and turn it around Oddly enough, thinking of a counterargument can often help you to see the assumptions beneath an argument you are inspecting. For example, say that you hear a senator arguing that taxes should go up because we need to pay off the national debt. How to figure out a major assumption here? If you know a different argument, that taxes should not be increased because keeping taxes low will encourage businesspeople to make and sell more products which government can tax, thus collecting more money, you can argue that the senator may be assuming that keeping the tax rate low will *not* stimulate business sufficiently to reduce the national debt. You took the reason for the second argument and put a "not" in front of it. Or if someone else argues that we don't need to pay off the debt because it has no effect on the economy, you can say that the senator seems to assume that paying off the national debt *would help* the economy.

This technique, of turning the reason of an alternative argument around, may explain why it is easier to locate assumptions beneath arguments we don't agree with. Discovering one's assumptions can be a delightful or unsettling surprise, and it often leads to an enlarged understanding.

Seek the Pivotal Term

Let's examine this standard argument:

Abortion is murder because it involves the killing of a fetus.

Is there a word that does most of the persuading here? If you were going to counterargue, with which word would you most take issue? Underline it.

Definitions for the terms "abortion," "killing," and "fetus" could probably be found to meet the approval of both pro- and anti-abortionists. But what about murder? "Murder" is defined as the unlawful killing of one *human being* by another.[1] From this definition we can see that the arguer is assuming that a fetus is a human being rather than merely human tissue (otherwise it couldn't be murder).

The standard counterargument runs as follows:

A pregnant woman is morally entitled to exercise choice and abort the fetus.

In light of the term "human being," what would you suppose that this side is assuming about the fetus? The assumption is probably that the fetus is merely human tissue, a potential human being rather than an actual one. To claim that the pro-choice advocate *probably* assumes that the fetus is not an actual human being is to hedge, because almost everyone in our society assumes that all human beings have an equal right to life: One human being has no right to kill another human being.*

Unearthing assumptions engages arguments All of this additional insight into the abortion example came from careful investigation of the pivotal term, "murder." But where is it getting us? *Both arguments are forced into closer communication.* You'll realize that this is no small feat if you've noticed how polarized the arguments about abortion often are. Now the pro-life side has to convince the pro-choice side that a fetus is a human being by appealing to some evidence that clinches the issue; for example, "The fetus has a heartbeat by the fifteenth day, so it must be a human being at that time." The pro-choice side for its part must convince the pro-lifers that a fetus is not (yet) a human being; for example, "Brain function and the capacity for suffering don't appear until the fourth month, so it's not human until that point." Do you notice that concessions have been imaginatively wrung from both sides?

Practice with pivotals See if there's a pivotal word in the following argument:

> Education is merely a subtle form of manipulation. Students are encouraged to acquire a certain set of facts and values, with grades constituting reward or punishment, depending upon how well a particular student has been conditioned.

Presumably, nobody has trouble understanding "education," in the sense of schools, classes, etc. The same applies to "grades"; good grades are rewards, poor grades are "dings" for not being up to snuff. One pivotal term here is "manipulation." Another is "conditioned," which is a synonym for manipulation. These terms carry the weight of the argument. Both the counterarguer and the arguer will need to give a careful definition to that term "manipulation," convincing the other side that it does or does not fit into the larger definition of education.

In sum, the discovery of pivotal terms uncovers definitional assumptions, clarifies arguments, and gives counterarguments a chance to engage

*It is fascinating to learn how many cultures have not acted out of this assumption that all members have an equal right to life. Of course, it is always possible to consider the fetus to be a human being yet sanction aborting it on the grounds that a woman's freedom from the burden of birthing is more important than the life of a human being. I would assume this position is rare.

one another more directly. Pivotal terms are trap doors through which you can fall to the basement. And once you're down there and can see what is shoring up a controversial argument, you realize that those particular assumptions need *not* necessarily be made; without explicit awareness of assumptions, it is all too easy to accept them without even being aware of it. Pivotal terms occur frequently in arguments, and you should be on the lookout for them.

Values Assumptions

Many arguments proceed on the assumption that one value is more important than another. Here is a brief list in which the terms can be switched (e.g., an argument can assume that social order is of greater value than political freedom):

ASSUMES THAT . . .	IS OF GREATER VALUE THAN . . .
political freedom	social order
personal gain	consideration for others
social harmony	personal expression
equality of opportunity	racial quotas
seriousness	humor
leisure time	making more money
thrift	generosity

Did you spot any possible false dichotomies? Did you wish that some of these terms were defined?

Don't fall into the pat answer, "All of these things are valuable." Perhaps they are. But the important question is how much of which under what precise circumstances.

What values assumptions are predominant? Have you ever caught yourself operating out of an assumption which you had never even considered? It is really an eye-opener to discover these assumptions. The following assumptions were held by many people in the past two decades. Do you agree with them, and do you think that most people accept them these days?

The new, the shocking in art is more valuable than the traditional.

Social forces shape the individual more than he shapes himself.

Values are relative to time and culture, not absolute.

Sunday-Monday syndrome Very different arguments are erected on diametrically opposed values assumptions. What is interesting is catching ourselves believing both. For example, on Sunday someone barges in front of you in line. You mentally argue, "Oh, well, forget it. That person just wasn't paying attention, and probably has lots of problems." Sunday's assumption: The best way to live is to turn the other cheek. On Monday someone barges in front of you in line. You mentally argue, "What nerve! That so-and-so can't do that to me; I was here first." Monday's assumption: The best way to live is to stick up for your own rights.

Unexamined values assumptions tend to make beliefs and decisions automatic. (It can be assumed that that's bad.) Because we live in a pluralistic society, we have more opportunity to encounter people with different values assumptions (and as long as those values don't include harming others, it can be assumed that that's good).

Factual Assumptions

We make arguments and base decisions not only on what we believe should be, but on what we believe *is*, the case. Here are some examples of factual assumptions examined in the language of argumentation:

> I would agree with the **author's assumption that in fact . . .**
> The author **is assuming that** in expressing anger one will get rid of it; **in fact,** studies have shown that . . .
> Is the author **assuming that . . . is in fact the case?**
> I would **question the assumption that . . .**
> This argument **rests on the assumption that . . .**

Sometimes you will read, "The underlying assumption is that," but since assumptions by definition "underlie," the word is redundant.

Assumptions take the most work, but are worth it Unearthing assumptions is a skill that takes more practice and thought than any of the other twelve basics of critical thinking. Beginners often claim that the reasons of an argument are its assumptions (and sometimes in informal conversation reasons *are* called assumptions, just to complicate matters). But assumptions should cast a new light on the argument, not rehash the argument or be irrelevant to it. It is fascinating that in any group of people digging up assumptions, some will come up with assumptions that you would never have thought of—a piece of evidence for the importance of the community of thinkers.

IMPLICATIONS

The press uses "implicate" in its most lurid incarnation: to be involved intimately or incriminatingly, as when a newspaper informs us that someone is involved in a scandal. "Rock Star Implicated in Affairs with Twenty Cocaine Dealers," it blares.

But in its older, more interesting sense, "implication" means to interweave or entangle; entwine. We constantly entangle ideas. Implication has come to mean the way a conclusion might affect (entangle) other areas outside the argument. Here is an example:

> As long as women continue to work, the American family will remain small. For the first time in many generations, there will be far fewer people under eighteen years. **The implications** of this demographic change **are numerous.** As the average age rises, everything from advertisements to government policy will change to cater to this aging majority.

An implication is often a *practical upshot,* or outcome, of a conclusion. The foregoing passage argues quickly to the conclusion that there will be fewer children, then goes on to explore the outcome of this conclusion for society at large. The implications discussed might be favorable or unfavorable. When the implications are positive, they function as additional reasons for an argument.

But implications can also be negative, neutral, or unclear. It is not clear, for example, whether the writer above thinks that such catering to the majority is a good thing.

Or say that you are arguing against increased taxes, claiming that one implication of heavier taxation would be the bankrupting of many small businesses. This is an unfavorable implication and one that could be offered as a reason in a counterargument.

Remember that implications arise *beyond the main argument at hand.* They are additions to an argument's main reasons. Implications should be easy to spot, because when they're mentioned, they are identified.

Language

> **The implications** for the atmosphere from tropical deforestation **are immense.**
> **There are a number of implications** to this idea.
> **Important implications are at stake** with this argument.

Here's another example of implication: Say that you're an unemployed computer whiz who worked hard to become skilled at writing. You find the following claim in a computer magazine:

> Informal surveys indicate that the average microcomputer owner buys nine to twelve books about that computer within six months of purchase.

What might the financial implications be for you? What other implications might there be for publishing houses, businesses, or others? If you hit upon the possibility of writing a book about microcomputers, then you *saw an implication* in the facts that you were given.

Notice that these implications are just possibilities—you haven't collected your royalties yet. Implications are usually predictions whose truth has yet to be established. Furthermore, implications can themselves become conclusions of different arguments, with all the same structural properties of arguments (e.g., it is arguable whether advertisements would change to cater to an aging population).

SUMMARY

Assumptions Defined

A student came up with a clever definition of assumptions: "the (hidden) reasons for the reasons given in an argument."

Look for the following:

1. pivotal, significant terms
2. alternative arguments whose reasons you can turn around

Types of Assumptions

1. values assumptions
2. factual assumptions

Assumptions are hidden unless stated as such.

Implications Defined

Implications are possible outcomes that follow from an argument. Unless explicitly mentioned, they are factors outside of the argument at hand.

EXERCISES

1. What is assumed by the claim that criminals can be rehabilitated by being put in a humane environment?
2. What is assumed by the claim that a humane environment won't rehabilitate criminals?
3. Consider the adages, "Good guys finish last," and, "Give them an inch and they'll take a mile." What is assumed in these proverbs about human nature: Is it good, bad, or neutral?
4. Can you think of other adages that make assumptions about human nature?

5. Answer the following, giving values and factual assumptions if you can. What do most Democrats assume about taxing the wealthy? What do Republicans generally assume about it?
6. List all possible implications you can think of if intelligent beings from another galaxy were to come for a visit. (Do a number of implications hinge on some important fact about these beings?)

READINGS

1. There are numerous assumptions beneath any given argument, for instance, that the world exists, that the argument in question exists, and that argument is a valuable way to persuade. Some philosophers, concerned about this vast basement full of hidden assumptions and their effect on arguments, have claimed that we should try to construct arguments with few or no assumptions. Karl Popper counters this argument by pointing out its own "colossal assumption":

> Since all argument must proceed from assumptions, it is plainly impossible to demand that all assumptions should be based on argument. The demand raised by many philosophers that we should start with no assumption whatever . . . and even the weaker demand that we should start with a very small set of assumptions ('categories') are both in this form inconsistent. For they themselves rest on the truly colossal assumption that it is possible to start without, or with only a few assumptions, and still to obtain results that are worthwhile.[2]

2. Even arguments that discuss assumptions have still more hidden assumptions. What assumptions remain hidden in this argument?

Some Pernicious Assumptions About I.Q.

Many people reason as follows: "I studied hard but didn't do well on that test, so I must not have the mental ability to do well in that subject." This argument is based on the questionable assumption that each person is endowed with a fixed mental ability, some people having more, and others (always including the person worrying) having far less.

I.Q. was never meant to measure "mental ability." I.Q. is merely a measure of how schoolchildren are *achieving* vis-à-vis children their age. I.Q. is totally meaningless for adults (presumably because everyone is learning something different). Further, since test-taking is inextricably bound up with an individual's motivation toward, and past exposure to, a subject, it is also meaningless as a measure of a child's ability, only measuring that child's achievement as compared with the achievement of other children that age in that subject area.

A far more pleasant assumption would be that most people are born with almost equal mental abilities. Then motivation, self-confidence, and opportunity to learn are the operant factors in the different performances among most people.

This assumption probably has no firmer evidence to support it than does the notion of a large range of innate abilities among people. But the implications of accepting the "equality" assumption are vastly different from the "innate-range-as-measured-by-I.Q." assumption.

The implications of concluding that each time one fails one has overreached his mental abilities are that this person will not continue to strive in that area. The person's feeling of inadequacy may spread to other endeavors as well.

On the other hand, if a person regards himself as having the same mental abilities as those who succeed in a subject, he will suppose that he did not have enough exposure to the subject or wasn't properly motivated. Not only is there considerably less sting to this interpretation, but the person is far more likely to try again, and harder. The implications for a happier, more striving society are clear if more people would operate out of this assumption of general mental equality.

3. This is a stunning argument by Margaret Visser, not because of its unusual structure (which is one conclusion with a mass of evidence), but because it points to the overwhelming use of corn in our society. What implications can you imagine flow from this argument?

You cannot buy anything at all in a North American supermarket which has been untouched by corn, with the occasional and single exception of fresh fish—and even that has almost certainly been delivered to the store in cartons or wrappings which are partially created out of corn. Meat *is* largely corn. So is milk: American livestock and poultry is fed and fattened on corn and cornstalks. Frozen meat and fish has a light corn starch coating on it to prevent excessive drying. The brown and golden colouring which constitutes the visual appeal of many soft drinks and puddings comes from corn. All canned foods are bathed in liquid containing corn. Every carton, every wrapping, every plastic container depends on corn products—indeed all modern paper and cardboard, with the exception of newspaper and tissue, is coated in corn.

One primary product of the maize plant is corn oil, which is not only a cooking fat but is important in margarine (butter, remember, is also corn). Corn oil is an essential ingredient in soap, in insecticides (all vegetables and fruits in a supermarket have been treated with insecticides), and of course in such factory-made products as mayonnaise and salad dressings. The taste-bud sensitizer, monosodium glutamate or MSG, is commonly made of corn protein.

Corn syrup—viscous, cheap, not too sweet—is the very basis of candy, ketchup, and commercial ice cream. It is used in processed meats, condensed milk, soft drinks, many modern beers, gin, and vodka. It even goes into the purple marks stamped on meat and other foods. Corn syrup provides body where "body" is lacking, in sauces and soups for instance (the trade says it adds "mouth-feel"). It prevents crystallization and discolouring; it makes foods hold their shape, prevents ingredients from separating, and stabilizes moisture content. It is extremely useful when long shelf-life is the goal.

Corn starch is to be found in baby foods, jams, pickles, vinegar, yeast. It serves as a carrier for the bubbling agents in baking powder; is mixed in with table salt, sugar (particularly icing sugar), and many instant coffees in order to promote easy pouring. It is essential in anything dehydrated, such as milk (already corn, of course) or instant potato flakes. Corn starch is white, odourless, tasteless, and easily moulded. It is the invisible coating and the universal neutral carrier for the active ingredients in thousands of products, from headache tablets, toothpastes, and cosmetics to detergents, dog food, match heads, and charcoal briquettes.

All textiles, all leathers are covered in corn. Corn is used when making things stick (adhesives all contain corn)—and also whenever it is necessary that things should *not* stick: candy is dusted or coated with corn, all kinds of metal and plastic moulds use corn. North Americans eat only one-tenth of the corn their countries produce, but that tenth amounts to one and a third kilograms (3 lb.) of corn—in milk, poultry, cheese, meat, butter, and the rest—per person per day.[3]

NOTES

[1]*The American Heritage Dictionary* (Boston: American Heritage Publishing Co., Inc., and Houghton Mifflin Company, 1981), s.v. "murder."

[2]Karl R. Popper, *The Open Society and Its Enemies* (Princeton, N.J.: Princeton University Press, 1971), II, p. 230.

[3]Margaret Visser, *Much Depends on Dinner: The Extraordinary History and Mythology, Allure and Obsessions, Perils and Taboos of an Ordinary Meal* (New York: Collier Books, a division of the Macmillan Publishing Co., 1988), pp. 22–24. Reprinted by permission.

CHAPTER SEVEN

PRESCRIPTIONS

A FINAL TOUCH

Some arguments give an issue, reasons, conclusion—and stop there. Other arguments add a final touch in the form of a solution, usually a recommendation that something be done. Here's a brief example:

> The dramatic increase in deaths from teenage drunk driving leads to the inescapable conclusion that the problem of drunk driving in this population has worsened. Therefore, we believe that all advertising of alcohol should be banned.

The recommendation to ban advertising of alcohol is really an additional conclusion which goes beyond the basic conclusion that the problem of drunk driving among teenagers has worsened. This second conclusion forms a second, higher roof-line of an argument (see fig. 7.1).

In this type of argument, the solution usually lies at the end of the essay or book. If a solution is proposed at the beginning, chances are that the argument is purely prescriptive. Notice that you can agree with the argument without having to agree with the prescription, and vice versa.

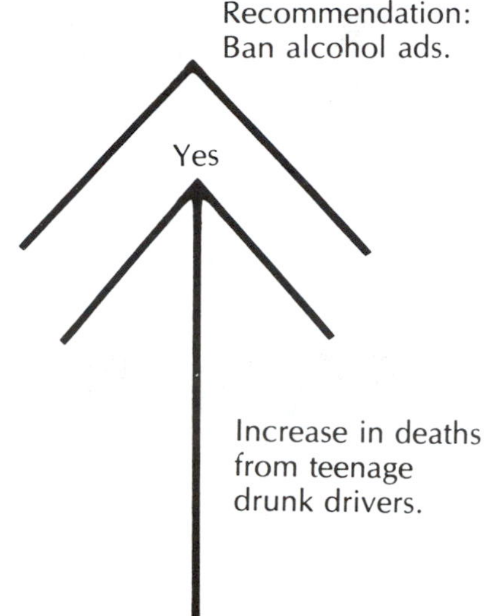

Issue: Whether drunk driving has worsened in the teenage population.

Figure 7.1

PRESCRIPTIVE ARGUMENTS

Unlike the foregoing, some arguments are all "final touch." Their *only* conclusion is a recommendation of what should be done. Their structure is just like that of the arguments we've seen in the five preceding chapters. In fact, a number of purely prescriptive arguments have been presented in those chapters. Do you remember them?

Prescriptive arguments are values arguments, telling us what *should* be done. At the opposite extreme lie descriptive arguments that claim that something *is* the case (see chapter 4).

Prescriptive Language

The solution seems to lie in . . .
The only way (or **one way) out of this dilemma is . . .**
The advice I would give for this problem is . . .
In light of the seriousness of the issue, the author **recommends that . . .**

Countering a prescritive conclusion:

It is arguable whether we should ban all alcoholic beverage ads. Although the author's argument is sound, **it is not a foregone conclusion that** her **prescription is the best** one.

Countering a factual conclusion:

> **It is arguable whether . . . is the case.**

Detached Advice

There are paragraphs, even books, full of loose arguments that are prescriptive. (For a review of factual claims and argument in the loose sense, see chapter 1.) Rather than being argument structures, these more closely resemble detached pieces of lumber:

> It's a good idea to marry later in life. Just keep company with a number of friends in your twenties, relax, and enjoy your youth. Don't worry that if you don't accept the first person who seems interested in you you'll have lost your chance for romance. That is just not true. Don't grab the first person who comes along. My advice is to wait until you're at least in your thirties, then get married.

This paragraph makes sense, and is built around the advice (here the conclusion) to marry in your thirties. But notice that the other sentences don't support the conclusion. They are *related pieces of advice* (i.e., tc have a number of friends, not to worry about finding a mate). If you try to turn these into reasons supporting the conclusion, it doesn't work: It's a good idea to marry later in life because you should just keep company with a number of friends in your twenties. While there is meaning and continuity of thought, one thought doesn't constitute a reason or get its support from another in that paragraph. On the other hand, watch this:

> It's a good idea to marry later in life. Too many people in their late teens and twenties don't yet know who they are and make fatal mistakes in choosing mates.

That is a brief formal argument. See the difference?

More Hybrids

For more evidence that life is complex, observe that much of what we read is a combination of strict and loose argumentation. A stack or two of descriptive or prescriptive lumber is followed by an argument, then perhaps more facts.

Sometimes a small argument nestles among a number of factual claims. See if you can find one here:

> In medieval society people generally blew their noses into their hands, just as they ate with their hands. That necessitated special precepts for nosecleaning

> at table. Politeness, "courtoisie," required that one blow one's nose into the left hand if one took meat with the right. But this precept was in fact restricted to the table [in all other situations, people blew their noses into both hands]. It arose solely out of consideration for others. The distasteful feeling frequently aroused today by the mere thought of soiling the fingers in this way was at first entirely absent.[1]

In the midst of this colorful description, the author argues briefly that the reason for nose-blowing into the left hand at table was consideration for others.

SUMMARY

Some arguments contain a second conclusion, called the solution or prescription. The reader should evaluate the prescription on its own merits, separately from the conclusion.

Some arguments contain only one conclusion, which happens to be prescriptive.

Sometimes arguments nestle among factual claims.

EXERCISES

1. Take any three arguments presented in the first six chapters and invent a prescription that is consistent with each of the arguments.
2. Make a formal argument that detached pieces of advice are not as valuable as formal arguments. Include a prescription in your argument.

READINGS

1. Bertrand Russell has some wonderful advice about how to avoid feeling envy:

> Of all the characteristics of ordinary nature, envy is the most unfortunate; not only does the envious person wish to inflict misfortune and do whatever he can with impunity, but he is also himself rendered unhappy by envy. Instead of deriving pleasure from what he has, he derives pain from what others have. If he can, he deprives others of their advantages, which to him is as desirable as it would be to secure the same advantages himself. . . . Fortunately, however, there is in human nature a compensating passion, namely, that of admiration. Whoever wishes to increase human happiness must wish to increase admiration and to diminish envy.
>
> What cure is there for envy? . . . The only cure for envy in the case of ordinary men and women is happiness, and the difficulty is that envy is itself a terrible obstacle to happiness. . . .
>
> Merely to realize the causes of one's own envious feelings is to take a

long step towards curing them. The habit of thinking in terms of comparison is a fatal one. When anything pleasant occurs it should be enjoyed to the full, without stopping to think that it is not so pleasant as something else that may possibly be happening to someone else. "Yes," says the envious man, "this is a sunny day and it is springtime and the birds are singing and the flowers are in bloom, but I understand that the springtime in Sicily is a thousand times more beautiful, that the birds sing more exquisitely in the groves of Helicon, and that the rose of Sharon is more lovely than any in my garden." And as he thinks these thoughts, the sun is dimmed and the birds' song becomes a meaningless twitter and the flowers seem not worth a moment's regard. All the other joys of life he treats in the same way. "Yes," he will say to himself, "the lady of my heart is lovely, I love her and she loves me, but how much more exquisite must have been the Queen of Sheba! Ah, if I had but had Solomon's opportunities!" All such comparisons are pointless and foolish; whether the Queen of Sheba or our next-door neighbor be the cause of discontent, either is equally futile. With the wise man, what he has does not cease to be enjoyable because someone else has something else. Envy, in fact, is one form of a vice, partly moral, partly intellectual, which consists in seeing things never in themselves but only in their relations. I am earning, let us say, a salary sufficient for my needs. I should be content, but I hear that someone else whom I believe to be in no way my superior is earning a salary twice as great as mine. Instantly, if I am of an envious disposition, the satisfactions to be derived from what I have grow dim, and I begin to be eaten up with a sense of injustice. For all this the proper cure is mental discipline, the habit of not thinking profitless thoughts. . . . You can get away from envy by enjoying the pleasures that come your way, by doing the work that you have to do, and by avoiding comparisons with those whom you imagine, perhaps quite falsely, to be more fortunate than yourself.[2]

2. Find the formal argument(s) in this advice to keep a budget, delivered in delightful style:

If you do take the time to plan your financial future and to track your progress as it unfolds, don't be slavish about it. Who cares if you forget to jot down every last expense? Who cares if you go over budget from time to time? The idea isn't to account for every penny (although it would be an intriguing experiment for three months to see exactly where the money goes). The idea is to spend less than you earn each year, get out of debt, and build a secure, comfortable future.

The trick is to live a little beneath your means. Sounds glamorous, no? Okay, no. But if, earning $23,000 a year, you can force yourself to live as if you were earning $18,000 or $20,000 (people do, you know); or if, earning $140,000, you can live as if you were making $115,000—your life in the long run will be far more secure and, soon, more comfortable to boot. Your money begins to work for you, your savings swell, and you can pay for things with cash. The other way, living a bit above your means, you get deeper and deeper into hock, and life costs an extra 18% in finance charges. One way you're motivated by the carrot (saving up in great anticipation of whatever it is you're saving up for), the other way by the stick (having to pay for it—even though it wound up raining the whole time you were there).

Living beneath your means is tough. (Living *within* your means is tough!) Making a game of it helps. Seeing it as a challenge helps. "Paying yourself first" helps (direct the first 10% or 15% of every paycheck to a savings account or mutual fund). But tough as it is, as you begin to see results, it gets easier. And if you want to get ahead of the game, you're more likely to succeed this way than by buying lottery tickets each week, hoping to win big.

One way or another, the future will come. With a little planning, you can have a say in how it looks. Even the difference between coming out just $500 ahead each year rather than $500 behind is the difference, for a 25-year-old who earns 8% after tax on his savings or borrows at 12%, between having $57,000 at age 55—or owing $120,000.

Think of your budget not as your albatross, but as your secret weapon.[3]

3. Is the following passage prescriptive, in your opinion? Is it an argument in the loose or strict sense?

Basically, I require two things of an author. The first is that he have something interesting to say—something that will either teach me or amuse me. If he doesn't I stop reading. The second requirement is that he not waste my time getting out what he has to say. If he idles, I conclude that I can be taught quicker elsewhere.

Beyond these two basic requirements, what I find most appealing in a writer is an authentic personal manner. I like to see him come across as a living, companionable human being, not as an emotional eunuch or stuffed shirt. I like to have an author *talk* to me, unbend to me, speak right out to me. If his prose has a natural, conversational rhythm to it, if it's forged out of basic, idiomatic English rather than pretentious Highbrow English, if it's stamped with the mark of his quirky personality, if it carries the ring of honesty and passionate conviction, then he's my man. What I'm saying, I guess, is that I like an author to be himself, warts and all. It shows me that he trusts me with his vulnerability, isn't afraid of me, and isn't afraid of himself either.[4]

NOTES

[1]Norbert Elias, *The History of Manners, The Civilizing Process* (New York: Pantheon Books, a division of Random House, Inc., 1978), 1, p. 148.

[2]Bertrand Russell, *The Conquest of Happiness* (New York: Bantam Books, a division of Grosset & Dunlap, Inc., 1968), pp. 56–59.

[3]Andrew Tobias, *The Only Other Investment Guide You'll Ever Need* (New York: Simon & Schuster, 1987), pp. 32–33. Copyright © 1987 by Andrew Tobias. Reprinted by permission.

[4]John Trimble, *Writing with Style: Conversations on the Art of Writing* (Englewood Cliffs, N.J.: Prentice-Hall, Inc., 1975), pp. 69–70.

CHAPTER EIGHT

CONSIDERING ALTERNATIVE ARGUMENTS IN LIGHT OF THEIR EVIDENCE

REVIEWING THE STRUCTURE

At this point you have learned all twelve fundamental argument features, as shown in figure 8.1. Not bad! If you had never thought in this way, you've greatly improved your critical thinking skills. The more you practice, the more adept you become.

Although the foregoing chapters touched on the evaluation of arguments, their major purpose was to help you get used to these twelve main features. Now that you know them, these next seven chapters will concentrate on judgment—how to build arguments and insulate them from holes.

EVALUATE BY COMPARING

Towards the end of Chapter 4, in the section titled "How Do You Evaluate the Evidence?," I mentioned that the best method is to watch for alternative arguments on an issue and to compare the evidence. This advice to "comparison shop" holds for the evaluation of any argument. **Critical thinking is the consideration of alternative arguments in light of their evidence.**

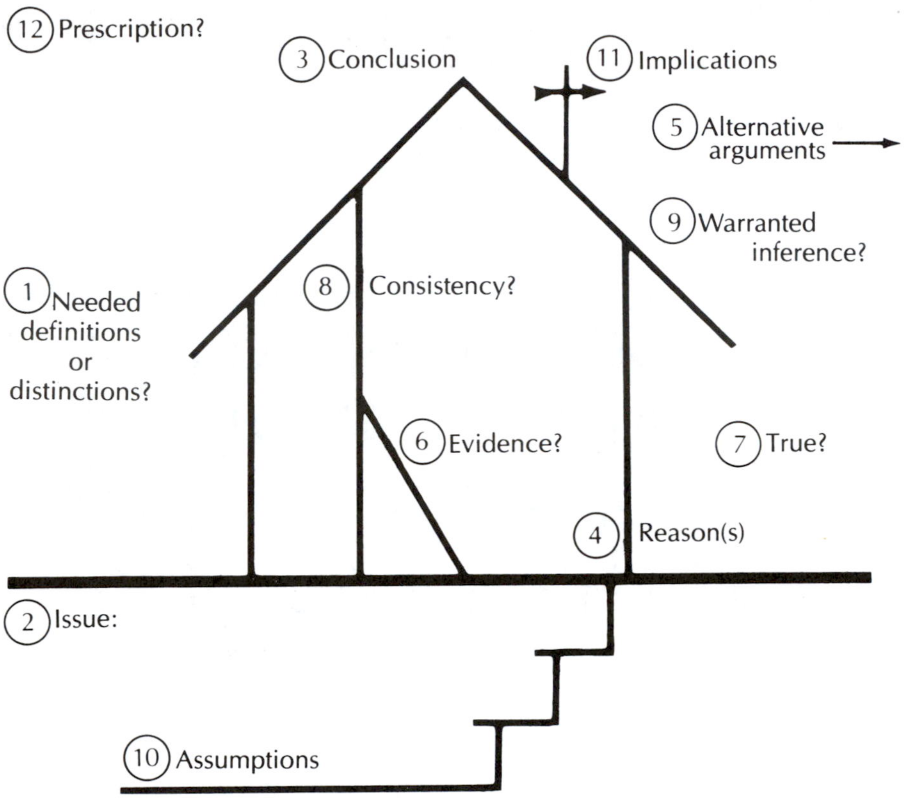

(12) Prescription?
(3) Conclusion
(11) Implications
(5) Alternative arguments
(9) Warranted inference?
(1) Needed definitions or distinctions?
(8) Consistency?
(6) Evidence?
(7) True?
(4) Reason(s)
(2) Issue:
(10) Assumptions

Figure 8.1. The Twelve Basics

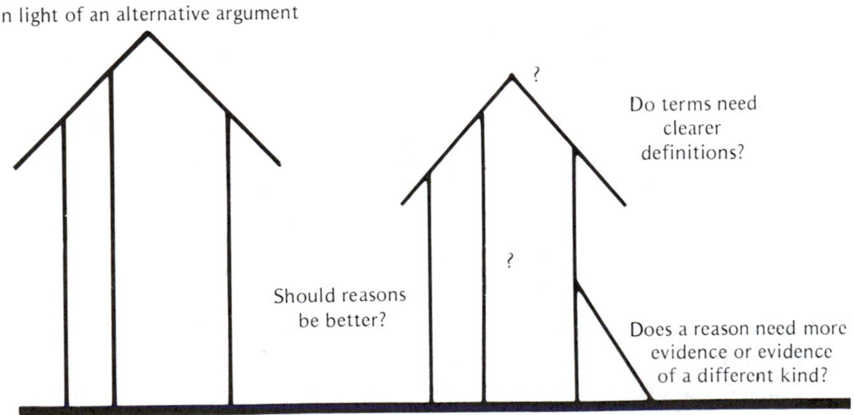

Figure 8.2

What if you don't know an alternative argument? At least stop for a minute and try to conjure one up (this gets easier with practice, wide reading, and age).

MAJOR EVALUATIONS: BETTER, CLEARER, MORE

With your understanding of argument structure, think of how an argument could be made more persuasive in light of an alternative. Three major evaluative terms are "clearer," "better," and "more." Could an argument, say, define "justice" or "pleasure" more clearly than it does, thus comparing more favorably to comparable arguments that you know? Likewise, could the argument be strengthened by better reasons or more evidence in light of your knowledge of alternative arguments, or spell out implications more clearly (see fig. 8.2)? Like insulation, "clearer," "better," and "more" can be used anywhere that you think they're needed in the structure.

BE EXPLICIT

The more helpful you can be to an argument, the better your criticism. For instance, rather than stopping with the easily made remark,"That argument needs better reasons," be helpful by actually coming up with better reasons:

> That argument **could be supported by better reasons, such as . . .**
> **There are more central reasons is favor of the argument. They are . . .**
> Hacker's argument **needs better substantiation in the form of** careful cross-cultural studies.

If possible, go on to explain why your reasons are better:

> **These reasons would provide better support for the author's conclusion, because . . .**
> **Such evidence would result in a stronger argument, because . . .**

This same explicitness should be the hallmark of your suggestions for clarity. If you cannot understand the author, you should show what feature(s) of the argument you don't comprehend. If you think that a term is unclear, you should show by a distinction how it could be interpreted in two different senses, each of which alters the meaning of the argument. If you want additional reasons, evidence, or an explicit assumption, you should explain how these will help the argument.

WONDROUS ALTERNATIVE ARGUMENT

What if you think that the author should have offered more reasons, but you can't come up with any? Remember that an alternative argument or a counterargument can be quite revelatory of what could improve an argument. Consider the following:

> Modern technology, such as telephones, television, cars, and airplanes, has been a tremendous factor in uniting people and creating what has been called the "global village." Instead of communicating over a few hundred yards—the farthest that most people could afford to wander throughout the history of the world until this century—people now maintain communications over hundreds and thousands of miles.

But consider:

> The excellence of modern technology keeps people apart as never before. We are now so fixated by long-distance communication that most of us don't even know our next-door neighbor. We have lost the far more important and potentially supportive "local village" to the cold, anonymous "global village."

In light of each argument, it will be easier to see where the other needs fleshing out with "better," "clearer," "more." Perhaps your class could discuss these arguments and make helpful suggestions for both, then vote on which side convinces you more. For a review of counterarguments, see chapter 3.

DEFINITIONS FOR CLARITY

Don't forget the importance of defining the crucial terms in all arguments. By now you've noticed that good arguers do a lot of defining. "Define" comes from the Latin verb *definire,* to set bounds to. If bounds are not set for the more abstract terms, then we're all over the block rather than inside the one argument structure where we're supposed to be.*

*Edward de Bono argues that sloppy definitions can play a very important part in critical thinking at times, because they keep the mind free and creative. I'd be a bit more cautious to the extent of claiming that we should know when we are being sloppy and use sloppiness deliberately but not sloppily.

Don't Abuse the Request to Define

As always, balance and a sense of fairness are crucial. If one wished to be abusive, one could attack nearly all terms in an argument by going after the definitions ("What do you mean by '*attack*'?" "What do you mean by '*definition*'?") We've all probably done our share of irritating and stalling someone by this tactic. To the request to "Go study," for example, "What do you mean by 'study'?" The chances are excellent that the person responding was not in the least interested in the philosophy of education. The tack of asking for definitions should always be taken when you have the interests of truth in mind; but it should be taken *only* when you have the interests of truth in mind. So the desire to know the truth is a necessary and sufficient condition for requiring a more precise definition. For more on definition, see chapter 1.

TWO EXTREMES: NOVEL, UNNECESSARY

It is usually a compliment to say that an idea is novel. If an argument has unusual but relevant and persuasive reasons, by all means give it that compliment. If the reasons are not relevant, then they are unnecessary. Remember to think about what might be better removed from an argument (see chapter 1).

SUMMARY

Mulling over the major features of an argument, you should ask which of them could be better, more fully explored, or clearer.

A quick counterargument is an excellent tack for discovering what else an argument needs.

Don't abuse the request to define. Use it and all critical techniques with a will to get at the truth.

Critical thinking is the consideration of alternative arguments in light of their evidence.

EXERCISE

Is watching the news a waste of time or is it worthwhile? Use you knowledge of the twelve basics to make a rough draft of arguments on both sides. Identify the parts of the argument (reason, conclusion, etc.) in the margin. Then, using a different-colored pen, go back and improve on each argument in light of the other.

READINGS

1. No doubt you have noticed that arguments are messy. They are messy because, as indicated in chapter 3, arguers don't use the tools of argumentation in any prescribed order. Arguments are also messy in the sense that even good arguments leave themselves open to improvements in a lot of places.

   This disagreement between Eric and Sherry on advertising has many arguments and contains every critical thinking phrase in the book—almost. Follow along, noticing how each has to define and improve his or her arguments as a result of the other's response. Please do not assume that you should be arguing this well!

   Eric argues:

   Advertisements are in general misleading. Advertisers are notorious for misrepresenting their products to the public. For instance, how many ads have you seen in which the woman smoking is tall, slim, beautiful, and—as if that weren't enough—dressed gorgeously? **The implication is that** if you smoke, you will be all of these things too (unless you happen to be male, in which case you'll be instantly transformed into a handsome cowboy).

   Not only are the users of advertisers' products supposed to be beautiful people, but they are eternally happy. We are constantly treated to the sight of men and women in ecstacy over one product or another, be it dish soap or laxatives. Further, the images of men and women are often sexist: It's the woman who beams at her "whiter than white" wash, the man who delights in his brand of motor oil.

   Finally, **the most serious objection** to advertisements is the outright falsity of many of the claims made.

   Next, Sherry's argument:

   Advertisements are not in general misleading. Eric's argument is **based on a questionable assumption.** Is there a soul alive who seriously believes that he or she will be magically transformed into a beautiful woman or a cowboy upon lighting a cigarette? That would certainly be an **unwarranted inference.** Eric's particular **argument** against smoking advertisements **could be better if he offered** health reasons against such advertisements. But this argument against cigarettes **is not relevant to the issue whether** advertising is generally misleading.

   In what sense can it be said to be "misleading" for advertisers to show attractive people using their products? **Why must** an advertiser have to show normal or even unattractive people using a product? It's obvious that if someone who is "easy on the eyes" is demonstrating a product in a beautiful setting, we're more interested in watching. An advertiser should not be criticized merely for playing along with human nature.

   The **same type of counterargument applies** to images of happy people using a product. Since we all live on this planet, we know that not everyone is thrilled while using a scouring pad. But why criticize an advertiser for doing all she can to create a positive impression of her product—a "you'll-be-glad-that-the-grime-comes-off-easier" type of impression?

   The assumption beneath Eric's agrument is that an honest advertiser would show only the average user in an average situation. Some ads actually seem to do this, but **my point is that** they shouldn't *have* to show "average" people. Furthermore, **even if** the poor advertiser did show the average user of his product, he would **still** be subject to the criticism of sexism leveled by the argument above. So the advertiser is stuck in an impossible **contradiction:** should he show the "average" person (i.e., a woman) using a scouring pad, or should he adopt Eric's *nonsexist fantasy* and show a homely man using a scouring pad?

Eric's **point** that outright false advertising should be stopped **is well taken,** however. I agree that the FCC should fine or even imprison advertisers who make verbal fraudulent claims. I would, however, argue that such cases constitute a small percentage of all advertising.

In essence,* ads are attention-getting devices to remind people that certain products are for sale and that people should think about buying them. **Even granting that** ads create brief fantasies in order to get our attention, ads are not misleading, since we all know very well that they are just that: fantasies.

Eric comes back:

First of all, I think that the actual number of outright lies in ads is far greater than the "small percentage" that Sherry claims. On that issue, I guess we shall have to **agree to disagree** until we can **find some evidence for either case.** Even then, we may well need to discuss **how "lie" is defined** by those compiling statistics on the number of advertisers who lie about their products.

Now, regarding Sherry's **main argument** that ads are just "attention-getting" devices: This argument is naive. It **fails to take into account** the fact that advertising images have tremendous power to persuade and that this persuasion exists on both conscious and unconscious levels. So people are in fact misled into **the mistaken inference that** certain products are wonderful because beautiful and happy people are using them.

As far as the use of homely and unhappy people is concerned, I would argue that Sherry has **overstated my case.** It is not necessary for advertisers to show unattractive people. In fact, it is arguable that if an advertiser just showed a product being used in a normal manner by normal people, the ad would be so unusual as to cause a sensation. As things stand, however, advertisers are taking advantage of the public. Therefore, they are not acting in a socially responsible manner.

Sherry responds:

I disagree with Eric's claim that advertising images persuade on an unconscious level. Let's discuss conscious and unconscious persuasion separately and **see whether the distinction holds.**

To the extent that ads consciously persuade they are no more dangerous or pernicious than Eric himself, who is trying to persuade us to his point of view. **I assume that** we are both fully conscious at the moment!

Let's **more carefully define** "unconscious persuasion" by asking what, in fact, it would involve. **I infer that** if we were really persuaded on an unconscious level we would find ourselves buying mattresses and packs of cigarettes without having any inkling why we were doing so. Now, whom do you know who does that? No one in fact acts that way! I have never met

*This phrase often signals both a conclusion and a definition.

a person who has said, "I just found myself in the department store buying a sofa, and it wasn't until later that I remembered the furniture ad I saw the night before." While ads certainly *lure* a person to buy something, I believe that the temptation is conscious and I don't believe that ads ever overpower our will to resist their temptations. **The distinction between** being unconsciously persuaded **and** being tempted **is crucial to my argument.** My evidence is that no one is stepping forward and admitting to being overpowered. What most people who make this type of argument claim is that everyone *else* is being overpowered. Yet after seeing an attractive ad, as after any temptation, we can and do usually modify our desires with a little conscious thought.

Finally, Eric's argument **implies that** any ad is powerful enough to get me to buy. But I would **claim that this is not true.** If I am not interested in motorcycles, no ad in the world is going to "persuade" me out of hand to buy one. Other factors would have to come into play; for example, friends would be discussing getting motorcycles or I'd have to read that this was a great way to commute to work. And **to take the strongest case, if** I happen to think that motorcycles are quite dangerous, an ad showing glamorous people on motorcycles could not overpower my fears.

In sum, it is not clear that we can be unconsiously persuaded by any means, and certainly not by ads.

Eric responds:

I agree that people are not being misled in the crass sense that Sherry describes. Nobody walks away from the TV and into the motorcycle shop like a zombie. But that is not the type of influence I am talking about. Sherry **has created a false dichotomy between** conscious **and** unconscious states.

What I mean by "persuasion" is the daily bombardment of ads that eventually wears down our resistance to products and that turns us into the consumer culture that we have become. As Sherry says, no one steps forward and admits to being overpowered because we're not even aware of the influence that ads have on us!

Furthermore, Sherry's entire **counterargument is predicated on the false assumption that** everyone constantly acts just as rationally as *she* does (or perhaps, as she *thinks* she does). Hasn't she ever heard of hypnosis? Or Freud?

Sherry finishes up:

It seems that **the argument has shifted from** the question whether advertising is misleading **to the issue whether** one can be unconsciously influenced. The **argument** whether advertising misleads by an appeal to our unconscious now **hinges on the question whether** we can be unconsciously influenced. I think that there are important **differences between** advertisements, on the one hand, and hypnotic states and Freudian repression of traumatic events on the other. Frankly, the bald assertion that we are influenced but we don't know it is really odd. If we don't know that we were influenced, how can we be certain that we were, in fact, influenced? If Eric answers, "We know that we were influenced because we bought the sofa," then the reasoning is circular: We're influenced because we buy the sofa because we're influenced!

In any event, advertising is far closer to other "normal" events in life and is therefore no more persuasive than any other normal life event. I wonder what is **at the base of** this special condemnation of advertising—is it **predicated on the assumption that** free enterprise is itself evil? Or that wanting material things is evil?

As to the question whether the advertiser bears more responsibility than others to "mold" public attitudes toward sex roles, **I would suggest that it would be better** in the long run if advertisers reflected society's larger values about sex roles rather than attempting to create them. In fact, I think that's what advertisers do now. For instance, many advertisements reflect women having careers, men doing housework.

I doubt that ads influence people as much as Eric says, but especially if ads do have an unconscious effect, he should agree that we'd be far safer if advertisers restricted themselves to reflecting the values that society consciously holds.

2. Here is a novel argument about gossip by Sissela Bok. Can you make an alternative argument—say, *against* gossip—and use it to suggest ways that Bok could improve her argument (with "more," "better," or "clearer")?

Cheap, superficial, intrusive, unfounded, even vicious: surely gossip can be all that. Yet to define it in these ways is to overlook the whole network of human exchanges of information, the need to inquire and to learn from the experience of others, and the importance of not taking everything at face value. The desire for such knowledge leads people to go beneath the surface of what is said and shown, and to try to unravel conflicting clues and seemingly false leads. In order to do so, information (gossip) has to be shared with others, obtained from them, stored in memory for future use, tested and evaluated in discussion, and used at times to encourage, to entertain, or to warn. Everyone has a special interest in personal information about others. If we knew about people only what they wished to reveal, we would be subjected to ceaseless manipulation; and we would be deprived of the pleasure and suspense that comes from trying to understand them. . . .

Consider the many harmless or supportive uses of gossip: the talk about who might marry, have a baby, move to another town, be in need of work or too ill to ask for help, and the speculations about underlying reasons, possible new developments, and opportunities for advice or help. Some may find such talk uninteresting, even tedious, or too time-consuming, but they can hardly condemn it on moral grounds. . . .

Bok's argument grows more complex as she works out the distinctions she has in mind between harmless and harmful gossip. She claims that "three categories of gossip should be singled out as particularly reprehensible: gossip in breach of confidence, gossip the speaker knows to be false, and unduly invasive gossip." Although, as the author states, each of these involves uncertain borderline cases, most people would agree that betraying secrets and lying about others are immoral acts (though you're always entitled to disagree). But we need to know what "unduly invasive" means in order to distinguish it from the helpful kind of gossip-invasion, and that is where Bok is the most interesting. Notice the distinctions she makes while reasoning out "unduly invasive":

Is any gossip, then, unduly invasive whenever it concerns what is private, perhaps stigmatizing, often secret? If so, much of the gossip about the personal lives of neighbors, co-workers, and public figures would have to be judged inexcusable. But such a judgment seems unreasonable. It would dismiss many harmless or unavoidable exchanges about human foibles. . . .

How then might we sort out what is unduly invasive from all the gossip about private and secret lives? To begin with, there is reason to stop to consider whether gossip is thus invasive whenever those whose doings are being discussed claim to feel intruded upon. But these claims must obviously not be taken at face value. . . . While such claims should give gossipers pause, they are not always legitimate. People cannot be said, for instance, to own aspects of their lives that are clearly evident to others and thus in fact public, such as a nasty temper or a manipulative manner, nor can they reasonably argue that others have no right to discuss them. Least of all can they suppress references to what may be an "open secret," known to all . . . a topic treated in innumerable comedies about marital infidelity. Similarly, more concealed aspects of their lives may be of legitimate interest to others—their mistreatment of their children, for example, or their past employment record. . . . At such times, gossip may be an indispensable channel for public information.

Merely to *say* that gossip about oneself is unduly invasive, therefore, does not make it so. I would argue that additional factors must be present to render gossip unduly invasive: the information must be about matters legitimately considered private; and it must hurt the individuals talked about (e.g., result in the loss of a job).[1]

3. Read the following article, "Class Struggle: Should Schools Permit Searching of Students for Weapons, Drugs?" by Anne MacKay Smith. Locate the major arguments, and evaluate them.

Detroit high-school student Lynn Bittner says she was standing around with three of her friends outside school, waiting for their first class, when a policeman demanded their student ID cards. He herded them into the school security office, and without waiting for a woman security guard, stood them against the wall and frisked them.

"It was incredible. Thrown up against the wall like a criminal, when we hadn't done anything," Miss Bittner, 17 years old, says.

Students like Miss Bittner, who has since transferred to a Catholic school, dislike being subjected to searches. But not all searches are fruitless. Since the beginning of the year, special squads carrying metal detectors have found 59 guns and 69 knives and other weapons on Detroit students. Parents, concerned about their children's safety, generally support such efforts.

The situation in Detroit illustrates a dilemma faced by schools nationwide: how to protect students and the learning atmosphere without infringing on students' rights to be free of unreasonable searches. The issue is emotional. Proponents of the right to search note that when weapons are available, schoolyard scuffles have become matters of life and death.

Differing Views

"What's reasonable for someone standing on Main Street might be different from what's reasonable in school. We are dealing with children and the state has the responsibility to protect them," says Allan J. Nodes, deputy attorney general in New Jersey.

But Barry S. Goodman says, "The real issue is whether students shed their rights when they enter school." The two are arguing a New Jersey suit now before the U.S. Supreme Court as to whether a staffer's search of a teenager's purse constituted illegal search.

Until now, the courts haven't been of much help in resolving the conflicts. Rulings in dozens of cases have been complex and contradictory. Many school officials are hoping that the Supreme Court will lay some ground rules. The court is expected to rule in the New Jersey case before its term ends in July.

The case started when a Piscataway High School teacher found a girl, identified in the suit only as T.L.O., smoking in the bathroom, and an assistant principal demanded a confession. When T.L.O. refused, he checked her purse for cigarettes. He removed the cigarettes and saw rolling papers, then turned the contents of the purse over and found marijuana. The student was convicted of possession of marijuana with an intent to distribute it, and her appeal of that conviction is before the Supreme Court.

Issues in Appeal

At issue are whether the assistant principal had a right to search the girl's purse and whether the evidence obtained that way should be admissible in court. Mr. Nodes argues that it is, and that there should be a less stringent standard for searches in schools than elsewhere. But Mr. Goodman believes the search violated the most lenient standard for searches because there wasn't any reason for it: Smoking was permissible in some areas of the school, so finding cigarettes wouldn't have proved the girl was smoking in the bathroom. The plaintiff argues that suppression of the evidence would deter such illegal searches in the future.

Increasingly, schools and some courts have tried to carve out a middle ground between giving school officials full rights to search and the stricter "probable cause" standard for police officers, requiring that there be strong evidence to believe the person to be searched has committed a crime.

Search conflicts occur across the country. In Bridgeport, Conn., teachers are working to expand their right to search; teacher DeOla Jones Barfield says her interest was spurred by finding a high-school student carrying a gun in a gym bag. Nancy Demartra, a Louisville, Ky., fifth-grade teacher, says that there have been two shootings in city schools this spring and that teachers should have the right to search students and their property at any time.

But in the last two years, strip searches of students to find stolen money have prompted a spate of angry newspaper articles in Rockford, Ill., and two lawsuits in New York. Nationwide, dozens of suits have been filed questioning school searches.

Killings in Brooklyn

The debate as to when to search becomes most emotional when violence breaks out. Two students at the Samuel J. Tilden High School in Brooklyn, N.Y., were knifed to death in incidents six weeks apart this spring, the second in full view of students streaming out of the building after classes. Tilden, which prides itself on its academics and its winning football team, exploded with pleas from teachers, parents and more than 100 students that metal detectors be used to search students at the school doors.

Two weeks after the second death, the issue was heatedly debated at a meeting of the Parent-Teachers Association in the school's auditorium. Stephen Dorf, a resources teacher at the school, dismissed the civil-liberties concerns. "The good kids have to suffer with the bad sometimes. Sometimes we have to pick the lesser of two evils," he said.

But others argued that mass searches would erode students' rights.

"We will become the school that has our children pass through these portals and be presumed guilty. That is not the principle on which this society is founded," Agnes Green, president of the PTA, said. "I ask you to reconsider."

Mrs. Green says it took some agonizing thought to come to her position. She says she still worries about both physical danger to her 15-year-old son, and the scarring effect of close association with violence. As PTA president, she received early notification of the second stabbing, and she vividly recalls her son's reaction when she told him the victim had died.

"He said, 'You know, I figured as much, because of the way the blood was coming out of her body, and the way she fell to the sidewalk,'" Mrs. Green recounts. "Within a few weeks, my son has seen more death and destruction than I have in my whole life."

Her position against metal detectors seems to have triumphed. While the school has set up a task force to discuss ways to improve school security, metal detectors aren't likely to be one of them, the school's assistant principal says.

Parents of some third graders at P.S. 282 in Brooklyn sued school officials over a strip-search. They charge that the officials, who were looking for about $50 stolen from a substitute teacher's purse, stripped most of the class in spite of the fact that most of the stolen money was found on the first child they examined. Among the charges is that "all students who had been searched . . . were forced to stay outside the search chamber and listen to their classmates crying as they were being searched."

Two of the officials, a school guidance counselor and the district superintendent, filed a response in U.S. District Court in New York denying the allegations. Counsel for the school principal declined to comment on the charges, but said he believed the suit would be settled within a few weeks.

Richard Emery, a lawyer for the New York Civil Liberties Union representing the plaintiffs, says the effects of such a search are lasting, and that all searches are unsettling. "Very few of us can maintain a feeling of innocence and confidence when official authorities are searching, or even inspecting," he says. "The best people at maintaining a composed demeanor are usually the worst criminals."

J. L. Skelton, a senior at Detroit's Finney High School, has a scar at the side of his nose from a knife thrust during a school argument two years ago. Nevertheless, he agrees that the increased presence of security guards with metal detectors has a chilling effect.

"You could be walking by, and you don't have nothing, but you shut up, boom," he says. "I've seen plenty of students walking by using regular slang language, and they numb up. Go straight as a board."

Guards' Procedure

Security guards say they search only when they have "reasonable cause" to believe a student may be carrying a forbidden item. Causes might include smelling marijuana on a passing student, or a report, usually from another student, that someone is carrying a weapon.

But some students say that searches are less reasonable and more random than that implies, and they are aware that some are legally questionable. Suzanne Koten, a teacher at Detroit's Denby High School, says discussion erupted in her class on Basic Law when they began discussing search and seizure practices. "At that time, the police were in the building all the time, and the kids wanted to know why the police could just search them at any time," she recalls. "They feel that it's an infringement on their privacy to just be stopped like that. I do, too."

But students say weapons are common in Detroit schools. Finney senior Skelton says, "I know plenty of girls that have things on them—knives, box cutters, razors, scissors, nail files. As for the guys, some of them could sneak a .22 in here, any type of gun, if they really wanted to. I don't see how they could prevent it, unless you put bars on every door and every window."

Hiram McGee, a security guard in Philip Murray Wright High School, says he found a student making a gun stock for a rifle in woodshop class. He checked his locker and found all the other parts except the firing mechanism ready for assembly.

Self-Defense Argument

For students who live in dangerous areas, carrying weapons for self-defense is a way of life. In Detroit, some parents gave their children knives last fall after a number of girls were attacked and raped on their way to school.

Others say weapons are a status symbol, while Taris Jackson, a 17-year-old Denby student adds, "The reason some of them bring them is to protect things they've got on. Two-hundred-dollar chains, and $60, $70 track shoes. I said, why would you bring something that people would kill you to get, and they say they got to look sweet."

Lawrence Boyer, sharp-eyed after nine years as a guard in Detroit schools, has taken knives, drugs, and other contraband from dozens of students so far this year. At 10 paces, he spots a three-inch, cylindrical leather case, half-concealed in the hand of one of a stream of passing students. It holds a canister of Mace.

"You know you're not supposed to have this in school?" he asks.

"I need to get home!" the student exclaims. "There's two German Shepherds on my block. Loose," he emphasizes.

Nevertheless, Mr. Boyer impounds the Mace. In one hour and a half on duty, he tells a dozen students to take off their hats and asks eight others why they are in the hall during a class period. One student, who was trying to sneak back into the building after a trip outside, is taken to the assistant principal's office for a search. He is subsequently suspended for carrying 10 marijuana cigarettes.

Teachers' Perspective

Most teachers and principals believe that the threat of violence outweighs erosion of student rights. Arthur Jefferson, Detroit's superintendent of schools says he believes rights violations are kept to a minimum. But if they do occur, he says, "I'm not apologizing for that." He adds, "The stakes are too high, in our schools and in our community."

Paul Richards agrees. He is principal of Detroit's Philip Murray Wright High School, a normally quiet school that exploded in violence on April 19 that ended in a threat to Mr. Richards's life. It came from two brothers who were fighting with a former student and chased him into the school. There, at least 10 of the former student's friends joined the fray, wielding a hammer, nightsticks and umbrellas. The former student fled, guards captured one of the brothers, and the other was beaten unconscious. "When I got there, he was motionless, lying in a pool of blood," Mr. McGee, the security guard, says.

The violence may continue. "Supposedly, they have a contract out on me. I've been looking over my shoulder for the last few days, because you never know." Mr. Richards says. "I think that if they do it, it'll be a shooting, because there are so many guns around."

Not surprisingly, Mr. Richards is a proponent of strong measures to keep the schools safe. "Until we get serious about a few things, like handgun control, metal detectors don't bother me. If it keeps weapons out of the school, I'm for it," he says. "You have folks saying it's like a prison. But hell, if it saves one life, to me it'd be worth it."[2]

4. The Supreme Court announced its opinion on January 15, 1985. A majority of the justices held that searches of students could be conducted by school officials as long as they have reasonable grounds for suspecting that such a search will turn up evidence of a student's violation of school rules or of the law. The court found that the school officials had had reasonable cause to search T.L.O.'s purse for cigarettes; then the discovery of rolling papers gave reasonable cause to search further for marijuana. The justices held that all searches of students by school personnel fall under the protection of the Fourth Amendment, which guards against unreasonable search and seizure; yet school personnel are not subject to the strict standard of *probable cause* for search, only *reasonable cause.*

The following are excerpts from the justices' reasoning. Note the language of critical thinking:

A search of a child's person or of a closed purse or other bag carried on her person, no less than a similar search carried out on an adult, is undoubtedly a severe violation of subjective expectations of privacy.

Of course, the Fourth Amendment does not protect subjective expectations of privacy that are unreasonable or otherwise "illegitimate." . . . To receive the protection of the Fourth Amendment, an expectation of privacy must be one that society is "prepared to recognize as legitimate." . . . The State of New Jersey (appellate court from which this case came) has argued that because of the pervasive supervision to which children in the schools are necessarily subject, a child has virtually no legitimate expectation of privacy in articles of personal property "unnecessarily" carried into a school. This argument has two factual premises: 1) the fundamental incompatibility of expectations of privacy and the maintenance of a sound educational environment; and 2) the minimal interest of the child in bringing any items of personal property into the school. Both premises are severely flawed.

The justices conclude that children do have legitimate rights to privacy. Then they bring in the argument of the need for order:

Against the child's interest in privacy must be set the substantial interest of teachers and administrators in maintaining discipline in the classroom and on school grounds. Maintaining order in the classroom has never been easy, but in recent years, school disorder has often taken particularly ugly forms: drug use and violent crime in the schools have become major social problems. . . .

How then, should we strike the balance between the schoolchild's legitimate expectations of privacy and the school's equally legitimate need to maintain an environment in which learning can take place? It is evident that the school setting requires some easing of the restrictions to which searches by public authorities are ordinarily subject.

Some of the justices agreed only partially with the ruling. Justice Brennan felt that it gave school officials too much leeway, endangering students' right to privacy. He wrote a scathing rebuttal to the notion of the "balancing of governmental and private interests." Note the use of definition and distinction:

Today's decision sanctions school officials to conduct full-scale searches on a "reasonableness" standard whose only definite content is that it is not the same test as the "probable cause" standard found in the text of the Fourth Amendment. In adopting this unclear, unprecedented, and unnecessary departure from generally applicable Fourth Amendment standards, the Court carves out a broad exception to standards that this Court has developed over years of considering Fourth Amendment problems. . . .

I therefore fully agree with the Court that "the underlying command of the Fourth Amendment is always that searches and seizures be reasonable" [but hold that] seizures are reasonable only if supported by probable cause.[3]

Thus we have three different views: those of the appellate court, the Supreme Court, and Justice Brennan. The implications of the Supreme Court decision would seem to be that school officials have a freer hand in searching students but still have to be sure the searches are reasonable. Do you agree that this is a good idea? Why or why not?

NOTES

[1]Sissela Bok, *Secrets: On the Ethics of Concealment and Revelation* (New York: Random House, 1984), pp. 90–97.

[2]Anne MacKay Smith, "Class Struggle: Should Schools Permit Searching of Students for Weapons, Drugs?" *Wall Street Journal* (New York), May 30, 1984.

[3]*The United States Law Week,* "Opinion Announced January 15, 1985," The Bureau of National Affairs, Inc., Washington, D.C.

C H A P T E R

N I N E

HOW TO WRITE A DIALOGUE

BECOME TWO ARGUERS

Another excellent way to generate critical thinking, the consideration of alternative arguments in light of their evidence, is to write a dialogue.

With the twelve tools already at your disposal, you can construct some rather sophisticated arguments. Now try a kind of dual argument that, because of its greater density, reveals more about an issue than most arguments.

Chances are slim that outside of this class you will be required to write a dialogue. Yet dialogue-writing is a great tool for preparing a term paper and invaluable in making a personal decision, such as a career choice.

Think of a dialogue as consisting of two parties who disagree.* Both parties will come to life and flesh out their positions in your head. Call

*Dialogues can involve more parties who needn't disagree, but starting this way will help you to avoid pitfalls.

your characters A and B, or give them names if you want—but be careful not to get involved in dramatic details.

No writer knows how his or her dialogue will end. This is doubly the case in a well-constructed dialogue. Even as the author, you don't know how either side will progress—one side may convince the other, or a whole new approach to the issue may emerge. For the dialogue to work, you must argue equally strenuously for each side. Don't stack the deck on one side. This point cannot be stressed enough. Don't turn the dialogue into an interview, with one side feeding the other questions which the latter merely gives an opinion about. If that happens, the argument won't deepen and will, of course, be lopsided. Eventually A and B may have to agree to disagree on a point, but only after considerable skirmishing. What you're after is some sort of breakthrough into the deeper layers of the issue.

Think of the dialogue as a thin, tough, and tight construction. You will have several ideas on each side to throw into the ring. But hold back. Feed the ideas in one at a time and have both sides engage exhaustively over one idea before proceeding. Remember, you have no idea where the logic will take you—you have some ideas you think will tie in, but don't force them into the dialogue strand. Their time should arrive in the logical course of the dialogue. To feed ideas in one at a time, restrict yourself to one or two or, at most, three brief sentences per speaker.

Once A has stated a claim, B must directly counter that claim and support the counterclaim. Then A must come right back at what B has just said. Don't break the thread. Chances are you will be able to toss off three or four opening lines. Then, if you're really keeping the thought on target, you will get stumped for a time, and that is good. You'll wonder how on earth you're going to come back against that last brilliant point. Take a break and put the problem in the back of your mind for a while. Do something else and see what comes. Sometimes sleeping on it overnight will produce a mental breakthrough.

Finally, as you work keep rereading your dialogue from the beginning to ensure that you are staying on a consistent track. Don't get confused and switch your characters' positions!

Here is a summary of the rules:

1. A and B must *disagree*. Don't have one interview the other.
2. Keep each speaker's remarks *brief*.
3. Make each speaker *directly address* the point made by the last.
4. Don't lose your nerve. Adhere strictly to the first three rules; take frequent *breaks* when you get stuck.
5. Constantly *reread* the dialogue as you add to it.

A DIALOGUE

A. Boxing causes brain damage. It should be outlawed.

B. Nonsense! What evidence do you have that boxing causes brain damage?

A. Autopsies of professional boxers have revealed brain scarring. The condition is called "dementia pugilistica," otherwise known as punch-drunkenness, the symptoms of which are permanently slurred speech and slowness of thought.

B. I don't believe that you can measure "slowness of thought."

A. Why couldn't someone have given boxers problems of similar difficulty over a number of years and measured the time it took them to answer?

B. Perhaps the brain scarring does not cause the slurred speech and slow thought.

A. I assume that medical researchers did controlled studies, autopsying any number of nonboxers. Besides, if slurred speech and slowness of thought appear in virtually all professional boxers, and we already know that blows to the head cause brain damage, the inference that boxing causes brain damage seems warranted.

B. Let them wear helmets.

A. Helmets don't prevent this brain damage. Boxing could outlaw the hitting of a person's head.

B. That would ruin the sport!

A. That's what I assumed you and other boxing aficionados would say.

B. Well, even granting that boxing causes brain damage in some people, that's no reason to outlaw it.

A. How can you say that? You admitted that some people are damaging themselves!

B. People damage themselves all the time by doing things that we don't outlaw: They play football, they drink, they ride motorcycles—

A. Wait a minute—let's take those examples one at a time. First, football injuries are rarely brain injuries.

B. What's so sacred about a brain injury that makes it different from the lifelong paralysis suffered by a former football player?

A. It is the rare football player who suffers such a severe injury. It is the frequent boxer who suffers irreparable brain damage.

B. Look, there is frequent and irreparable damage to some part of the body involved in every sport: "Tennis elbow" is common among those professionals, chronic knee and foot injuries among runners. Do you suggest we also outlaw these sports because they injure people?

A. No! Brain damage is far worse than any other type of bodily damage, including paralysis.

B. You are overstating your case. The damage to a person's bodily movement in paralysis is severe; brain damage to boxers is comparatively minor.

A. How can you call slowness of thought and slurred speech minor injuries?

B. Well, it depends on what the boxer wants to do with the rest of his life. If he isn't in the business of writing dialogues or giving public speeches, he could live a very nice life with the millions he's made from the sport.

A. Look, how many boxers make millions? And even the, say, one in ten thousand boxers who does make a lot of money is going to need all his wits to decide how to invest and spend his money.

B. Oh, he can always hire someone to help him with that.

A. You seem to be assuming, B, that a boxer's mind is not a terrible thing to waste.

B. Not if the boxer doesn't care. A, you are just trying to impose your values on other people.

A. Of course; what are laws if not "values imposed on people"? Our criminal law imposes the value that people may not deliberately kill or injure one another, and boxing is a perfect instance of people injuring one another.

B. How is it different from wrestlers or football players injuring one another?

A. Boxing is the only sport that has as its object to damage the opponent's neurological system.

B. Oh, come on. Do you think that's what goes through a boxer's mind in the ring?

A. Those aren't his exact thoughts, of course. But to try to hit the opponent's head as many times as possible and ideally knock him out is to have as one's object the damage of the opponent's neurological system, even if a boxer doesn't realize that his acts will have a damaging effect.

B. But still—that damage isn't different from the neurological damage suffered in other sports.

A. B, you are stubborn. The plain fact of the matter is that far more neurological damage occurs from boxing, since that is the very purpose of the sport!

B. You're no slouch for stubbornness yourself. But another fact of the matter is that more deaths have occurred from football or hang gliding or horse racing than from the sport of boxing. Do you want to outlaw all of these sports because they violate your aforementioned value of our criminal law that "people may not deliberately kill . . . one another"?

A. Hm. But wait—you're not making an important distinction. If the intent of a sport were the death of opponents, were gladiator combats, then that sport should definitely be outlawed. But the intent in football is to put a piece of pigskin over a goalpost; that's not deliberate intent to kill.

B. You're not fair! The poor boxer is just out there trying to win, not trying to injure or to kill, and you want to outlaw his actions. But even though more deaths result from football you say you don't care as long as the football player is out there just trying to win. That's certainly inconsistent and unfair.

A. But don't you see? Boxing is set up with its central purpose that of injury. In football, injury and death are only occasional side effects of the central purpose of the game.

B. I don't see what "purpose" has to do with it. Results are results, and the number of deaths remains greater from football.

A. Purpose is central to the issue: In boxing, everyone is bound to suffer neurological damage; in football only a very few people die.

B. Are you then assuming that the death of a few people is less significant than the slight (O.K., moderate) brain damage of many?

A. I am assuming that any sport or activity in which brain damage is a certainty should be outlawed.

B. Then welcome to the prohibitionist cause! It's well know that alcohol kills brain cells, and every drinker suffers "neurological damage," your criterion for outlawing an activity.

A. You are failing to distinguish between the slight damage of the death of brain cells and the moderate to severe neurological damage resulting from boxing. The two are quite different in degree.

B. Well, this is where I need some information. If a person drinks a bottle of gin every day for twenty years, how serious is his neurological damage compared with that of a professional boxer?

A. In that case, I assume, the neurological damage would be severe. But the alcoholic is damaging himself; a boxer damages someone else.

B. That's a false distinction! Obviously both boxers in the ring are consenting to be hit, even though they hope they won't be damaged, just as the heavy drinker consents to drink, hoping, however irrationally, that damage won't result.

A. Your terms "consent" and "irrational" are intriguing. What if there were a law requiring placement of a "warning label" in a conspicuous place on all boxing equipment, describing the neurological damage that results from boxing?

B. I don't know how much boxing it would prevent, but a cigarette-type warning seems more just than prohibiting the sport altogether. Besides, outlawing boxing would create terrible enforcement problems.

A. Yes. I agree that the warning seems more equitable, since it respects freedom of choice. You've shown me that there are other activities people regularly engage in that harm them but are legal. Still, I think boxing should be illegal for anyone under twenty-one.

B. (groan) Here we go again.

Notice that the dialogue has moved forward and that both sides have come to a deeper understanding. But problems remain, one of which is raised at the very end.

Dialogue Dissected

Here is the same dialogue with the various moves explained. (Obviously, your moves are going to come in a different order when you write your dialogue.) Don't be misled; the moves were written the day after the dialogue was finished. You should likewise construct your dialogue and *then* analyze its moves.

A. Boxing cause brain damage. It should be outlawed.	Brief strict argument
B. Nonsense! What evidence do you have that boxing causes brain damage?	Truth of reason questioned
A. Autopsies of professional boxers have revealed brain scarring. The condition is called "dementia pugilistica," otherwise known as punch-drunkenness, the symptoms of which are permanently slurred speech and slowness of thought.	Evidence outlined
B. I don't believe that you can measure "slowness of thought."	Evidence questioned
A. Why couldn't someone have given boxers problems of similar difficulty over a number of years and measured the time it took them to answer?	
B. Perhaps the brain scarring does not cause the slurred speech and slow thought.	Debate over the likelihood that the evidence supports the claim of "brain damage"
A. I assume that medical researchers did controlled studies, autopsying any number of nonboxers. Besides, if slurred speech and slowness of thought appear in virtually all profes-	

Dialogue	Commentary
sional boxers, and we already know that blows to the head cause brain damage, the inference that boxing causes brain damage seems warranted.	
B. Let them wear helmets.	Solution prescribed
A. Helmets don't prevent this brain damage. Boxing could outlaw the hitting of a person's head.	Factual claim that this isn't a solution; solution prescribed
B. That would ruin the sport!	Implication
A. That's what I assumed you and other boxing aficionados would say.	
B. Well, even granting that boxing causes brain damage in some people, that's no reason to outlaw it.	Rejects A's original inference
A. How can you say that? You've admitted that some people are damaging themselves!	
B. People damage themselves all the time by doing things that we don't outlaw: They play football, they drink, they ride motorcycles—	Counterexamples
A. Wait a minute—let's take those examples one at a time. First, football injuries are rarely brain injuries.	Counterargues to the main point: brain injury
B. What's so sacred about a brain injury that makes it different from the lifelong paralysis suffered by a former football player?	Requests distinction
A. It is the rare football player who suffers such a severe injury. It is the frequent boxer who suffers irreparable brain damage.	Distinction between rarity and frequency
B. Look, there is frequent and irreparable damage to some part of the body involved in every sport: "Tennis elbow" is common among those professionals, chronic knee and foot injuries among runners. Do you suggest we also outlaw these sports because they injure people?	Counterexamples of frequent and irreparable damage from other sports
A. No! Brain damage is far worse than any other type of bodily damage, including paralysis.	Brain damage distinguished as worse

B. You are overstating your case. The damage to a person's bodily movement in paralysis is severe; brain damage to boxers is comparatively minor.	Claim that the damage is not in fact worse
A. How can you call slowness of thought and slurred speech minor injuries?	Reminder of definition of brain damage
B. Well, it depends on what the boxer wants to do with the rest of his life. If he isn't in the business of writing dialogues or giving public speeches, he could live a very nice life with the millions he's made from the sport.	Claim that seriousness of effect depends on a person's life-style
A. Look, how many boxers make millions? And even the, say, one in ten thousand boxers who does make a lot of money is going to need all his wits to decide how to invest and spend his money.	Argues that money is not a sufficient cause of economic security
B. Oh, he can always hire someone to help him with that.	Factual claim
A. You seem to be assuming, B, that a boxer's mind is not a terrible thing to waste.	Value assumption of B
B. Not if the boxer doesn't care. A, you are just trying to impose your values on other people.	Factual assumption about A
A. Of course; what are laws if not "values imposed on people"? Our criminal law imposes the value that people may not deliberately kill or injure one another, and boxing is a perfect instance of people injuring one another.	A agrees and justifies assumption by argument
B. How is it different from wrestlers or football players injuring one another?	Requests distinction
A. Boxing is the only sport that has as its object to damage the opponent's neurological system.	Distinction
B. Oh, come on. Do you think that's what goes through a boxer's mind in the ring?	Distinction questioned
A. Those aren't his exact thoughts, of course. But to try to hit the opponent's	Distinction made between sport's

head as many times as possible and ideally knock him out is to have as one's object the damage of the opponent's neurological system, even if a boxer doesn't realize that his acts will have a damaging effect.	purpose and athlete's intent
B. But still—that damage isn't different from the neurological damage suffered in other sports.	Denies distinction
A. B, you are stubborn. The plain fact of the matter is that far more neurological damage occurs from boxing, since that is the very purpose of the sport!	Factual claim
B. You're no slouch for stubbornness yourself. But another fact of the matter is that more deaths have occurred from football or hang gliding or horse racing than from the sport of boxing. Do you want to outlaw all of these sports because they violate your aforementioned value of our criminal law that "people may not deliberately kill . . . one another"?	Factual claim to refute claim that boxing is the most harmful sport
A. Hm. But wait—you're not making an important distinction. If the intent of a sport were the death of opponents, were gladiator combats, then that sport should definitely be outlawed. But the intent in football is to put a piece of pigskin over a goalpost; that's not deliberate intent to kill.	Intent in football distinguished from intent to kill
B. You're not fair! The poor boxer is just out there trying to win, not trying to injure or to kill, and you want to outlaw his actions. But even though more deaths result from football you say you don't care as long as the football player is out there just trying to win. That's certainly inconsistent and unfair.	Inconsistency
A. But don't you see? Boxing is set up with its central purpose that of injury. In football, injury and death are only occasional side effects of the central purpose of the game.	Purpose and side effects distinguished

B. I don't see what "purpose" has to do with it. Results are results, and the number of deaths remains greater from football.	Claim that results are more important than purpose
A. Purpose is central to the issue: In boxing, everyone is bound to suffer neurological damage; in football only a very few people die.	Distinction: many versus few
B. Are you then assuming that the death of a few people is less significant than the slight (O.K., moderate) brain damage of many?	Questions A's assumption
A. I am assuming that any sport or activity in which brain damage is a certainty should be outlawed.	A defines his assumption
B. Then welcome to the prohibitionist cause! It's well known that alcohol kills brain cells, and every drinker suffers "neurological damage," your criterion for outlawing an activity.	Claims implication of A's statement is that alcohol should be illegal.
A. You are failing to distinguish between the slight damage of the death of brain cells and the moderate to severe neurological damage resulting from boxing. The two are quite different in degree.	Distinction between damage to brain from alcohol consumption vs. boxing
B. Well, this is where I need some information. If a person drinks a bottle of gin every day for twenty years, how serious is his neurological damage compared with that of a professional boxer?	Request for fact; meant to eliminate distinction
A. In that case, I assume, the neurological damage would be severe. But the alcoholic is damaging himself; a boxer damages someone else.	Distinction
B. That's a false distinction! Obviously both boxers in the ring are consenting to be hit, even though they hope they won't be damaged, just as the heavy drinker consents to drink, hoping, however irrationally, that damage won't result.	False dichotomy

A. Your terms "consent" and "irrational" just gave me an idea. What if there were a law requiring placement of a "warning label" in a conspicuous place on all boxing equipment, describing the neurological damage that results from boxing?	Solution prescribed
B. I don't know how much boxing it would prevent, but a cigarette-type warning seems more just than prohibiting the sport altogether. Besides, outlawing boxing would create terrible enforcement problems.	Claims implications are uncertain, but agrees; implications for law enforcement
A. Yes. I agree that the warning seems more equitable, since it respects freedom of choice. You've shown me that there are other activities people regularly engage in that harm them but are legal.	Assumption exposed; consistency as reason to keep boxing legal
Still, I think boxing, like alcohol consumption, should be illegal for anyone under twenty-one.	Prescription
B. (groan) Here we go again.	

Try It

There are many points in the foregoing dialogue at which you may have thought, "A [or B] gave in too easily there; I would have said. . . ." Pick up the thread at that point and continue the dialogue in your own way.

SUMMARY

The dialogue is a tightly constructed argument/counterargument that is invaluable in plumbing any issue deeply.

The writer must make each side argue one point as strenuously as possible, exhausting that point before proceeding to the next.

The dialogue ends when the writer has thoroughly explored the major features of both arguments. The dialogue characters may end by coming to agreement, or they may still disagree—whatever the writer finds closer to the truth of the matter.

EXERCISES

Any of the topics covered so far in the book are, of course, grist for the dialogue mill. Here are some others. Use these to create your dialogues.

1. A. I want to get into the occupation where I will make the most money. In a choice between money and on-the-job contentment, I'll take the money.
   B. You should follow a career path that brings you the most happiness on the job. Obviously, making a decent salary will contribute to your happiness on the job, but it's better to take job satisfaction over money any day.
2. A. As a prerequisite for graduation, students should have to take basic education courses in all major subject areas. Otherwise, colleges are failing in their duty to students.
   B. I disagree. Forcing students to take certain courses destroys their natural incentive to learn.
3. A. Pornography is violence against women.
   B. That sounds ridiculous. "Violence" is defined as "physical force exerted for the purpose of violating, damaging, or abusing."[1] You may dislike pornography, but it certainly should be carefully distinguished from violence.
   A. I'm using "violence" in another of its definitions: "the abusive or unjust exercise of power; an outrage; a wrong."[2]

READINGS

Here are excerpts from two opposing points of view regarding population.

1. The first, "The Paradox of Population Growth," by demographer Robert W. Fox, emphasizes an explosive growth rate.

For most of mankind's history world population grew slowly, checked by epidemics, famine, and chronic malnutrition. Though the mortality rate was high, the birthrate was slightly higher, and with that small excess our numbers gradually increased.

Human population grows much like a savings account accruing compound interest—greater amounts yield greater amounts. English economist Thomas Malthus cited this fact in his 1798 "Essay on the Principle of Population," warning that human numbers—if unchecked—would soon outweigh the ability of the earth to feed them.

But Malthus was writing on the eve of a new era, when the industrial revolution would transform Europe. The continent's population did rise substantially during the 19th century as medical breakthroughs lowered the death rate, but simultaneous agricultural advances also allowed food production to rise. And emigration to America helped siphon off population excess.

The newly widened gap between birth and death rates gradually began to close as smaller families became socially acceptable. That trend quickened in industrialized countries during the 20th century, and today the gap between births and deaths is once again small.

In the developing countries a far different history prevails. Only in the 1930s did the death rate begin to fall, but it fell dramatically as imported technology improved overall health and dietary conditions. The birthrate, however, remained high. Its decline depends largely on changing cultural norms, and family planning has made substantial inroads only within the past two decades. As the gap between deaths and births widened, the population exploded. Generally speaking, there were not more births—there were more survivors.

With this considerable momentum, population expansion in these countries will continue. Even optimistic scenarios do not foresee a leveling off of growth until late in the 21st century.

Because the traditional birth-and-death-rate relationship has been broken in Third World countries only within the past few decades, they now hold very youthful populations, and the populations will continue to soar because there are more women of childbearing age. Hence the paradox of modern population growth: Even as the birthrate continues to fall, the population will rise.

For every 100 Africans today, 55 are under 20 years of age. Among Europeans, only 30 out of 100 are under 20. In 1975, 93 out of 100 African women were of childbearing age. The birthrate that year in Africa was 47 per 1,000, and 19 million children were born. The UN projects that by 2025 the African birthrate will fall to 25 per 1,000—a reduction of almost half. But by then the number of reproductive-age women will have risen to 430 million, and even with a lowered birthrate 42 million children will enter the world that year.

Rural Exodus Deepens the Crisis

[In the third world] the rural birthrate is consistently higher than the urban birthrate. As children grow and seek work, often their only choice is migration to a city. Most arable farmland is already under cultivation, and millions of small landholdings around the world can no longer be subdivided among large families. Often workers have no clear title to land, and primitive farming methods limit crop yield—and profit. . . .

The struggle to find work is all consuming in Third World cities, where combined unemployment and underemployment rates of 30 to 50 percent are common. Relatively few people find work in industry; the majority fill the service sector, where jobs range from clerical work, to hand-delivering messages across town in phone-poor cities, to washing windows of cars stopped in traffic. . . .

The World's Urban Explosion

The upsurge in Third World urban populations has overwhelmed resources. Sprawling slums, massive traffic jams, chronic unemployment, regular failure of electric and water services, strained educational and recreational facilities, and skyrocketing food and fuel costs are the stuff of daily existence.[3]

2. This excerpt from the book *Food First*, by Frances Moore Lappé and Joseph Collins, disavows the strong language of "explosion" and "crush," offering a somewhat different set of facts. How does the implied solution differ?

Are People a Liability or a Resource?

Terms like "tidal wave" and "inundation" can readily lead us to believe we are witnessing a natural and inevitable process [of unemployment-related hunger in the Third World]. Dramatic metaphors can jolt us by the very power of their imagery, but they can also lead us away from real understanding.

This question [whether people are a liability] reflects several widely held beliefs that we have found to be myths.

MYTH ONE: *Agriculture in underdeveloped countries is held back because there are just too many people in the countryside to be productively put to work.*

If too many workers per acre really stood in the way of production, wouldn't countries that have a *more* productive agriculture have *fewer* workers per acre than their less successful neighbors? Yet, what do we find? Japan and Taiwan, both thought of as agriculturally successful, have more than twice as many agricultural workers per acre than the Philippines and India. The value of production per acre in Japan is seven times that of the Philippines and ten times that of India. The overall trend, in fact, seems to show a *positive* relationship between the number of workers on a unit of land and the level of agricultural output. This may be hard for Americans to accept because we are taught to measure productivity in terms of how few people it takes to grow food. Such a measure makes no sense at all in underdeveloped countries with vast, untapped human labor resources. . . .

MYTH TWO: *Since agriculture cannot absorb any more people, the overflow from rural areas must go to the cities where new jobs in industry must be created for them.*

It was exactly this analysis of the problem that prompted both the neglect of agriculture and the promotion of industrialization by development planners during the 1950s and 1960s. The result? A lot of capital investment but remarkably few new industrial jobs. . . .

Foreign corporations with their labor-saving technologies . . . have aggravated the chronic "job crisis." Two hundred fifty-seven multinational corporations studied in Latin America employ less than one-half the number of people per unit of sales as do local companies. . . .A new modern factory employing a couple hundred persons might well put thousands of local craftsmen out of business. . . .

Efforts to solve the unemployment problem by creating jobs in centralized, urban areas are misplaced in any case. In underdeveloped countries agriculture and small-scale decentralized workshops serving the needs of local agriculture have the greater potential to absorb workers. China has been able to reduce the percentage of its workforce in full-time agricultural jobs. . . . This was accomplished not by creating urban industries but by developing small factories and workshops throughout the countryside to make farm implements and basic consumer goods. China's large rural, but nonagricultural, population also represents a sizable reserve labor force for agriculture [to help out at harvest]. . . .

Too Many People?

Measured globally, there is enough food for everyone now. The world is producing each day two pounds of grain—more than 3,000 calories and ample protein—for every man, woman and child on earth. A third of this grain now goes to feed livestock. . . . Thus, on a global scale, the idea that there is not enough food to go around simply does not hold up.

But global figures mean little, except to dispel the widespread notion that we have reached the earth's limits. What counts is whether adequate food-producing resources exist in countries where so many people go hungry. The resources do exist, we have found, but they are invariably underused or misused. . . .

According to United Nations Food and Agricultural Organization, less than 60 percent of the world's cultivable land is now being cropped. In both

Africa and South America less than 20 percent of the potentially arable land is cultivated. . . .

Barriers to unleashing this productive capacity are, in most cases, not physical; rather, they are economic: Wherever there is unjust, undemocratic control over productive resources, their development is thwarted.

In most countries where people are hungry, large landholders control most of the land. A study of 83 countries showed that slightly more than 3 percent of all landowners, those with 114 acres or more, control a staggering 79 percent of all farmland. But these large landholders are the least productive. Studies in seemingly diverse countries reveal that large landholders consistently harvest lower yields per acre than the smallest farmers. . . . Furthermore, many who hold large amounts of land for prestige or as an investment, not as a source of food, leave considerable acreage unplanted. . . .

In addition, low productivity results from economic and social injustices that obstruct agricultural improvements by small, poor farmers. . . . Moneylenders commonly charge the poor 50-200 percent interest. With no individual or shared ownership of the land, how can tenants, sharecroppers, and landless laborers either be motivated or have the wherewithal to conserve and improve the land for better crops? They realize any improvement will overwhelmingly go to advance the landowners, not themselves.[4]

Use the material in the two excerpts you have just read to continue the following dialogue.

A. The world is overpopulated.

B. It's overpopulated by insects, perhaps, but certainly not by people.

A. How can you say that when world population, which reached one billion in the early nineteenth century, went to two billion in 1930, and by the end of this century will top six billion?

B. You act as though the rate of growth will continue to increase. The birthrate has fallen, and the total number of people on this planet will peak and remain at the same level by the end of the next century.

NOTES

[1]*The American Heritage Dictionary* (Boston: American Heritage Publishing Co., Inc., and Houghton Mifflin Company, 1981), s.v. "violence."

[2]Ibid.

[3]Robert W. Fox, "The World's Urban Explosion," *National Geographic Magazine*, 166, no. 2 (August 1984), pp. 179–84.

[4]Frances Moore Lappé and Joseph Collins, *Food First: Beyond the Myth of Scarcity* (New York: Ballantine Books, a division of Random House, Inc., 1978), pp. 13–17, 24–27.

CHAPTER TEN

FOLLOWING COMPLEX ARGUMENTS

LIKE SIMPLE ARGUMENTS, LIKE COMPLEX

A complex argument is no different in its basic features than the simple ones we've looked at so far. It has the basic three and most, if not all, of the other main features we've investigated. The difference is that a complex argument is a larger structure, containing smaller arguments whose conclusions usually function as the reasons for the complex argument. The smaller arguments are called "subarguments" (see fig. 10.1).

The easiest way to follow complex arguments is to locate the overarching issue, conclusion, and reasons, saving any details of the subarguments for later.

Three Examples

Consider the following argument:

> The Latin democracies cannot repay their debt. The high price of oil in 1973 and the hope of economic development caused Argentina, Brazil, Venezuela, Mexico, and Peru to borrow billions of dollars from U.S. and European banks at high interest rates. Despite heroic efforts, these countries cannot repay this $1.3 trillion debt as it now stands.

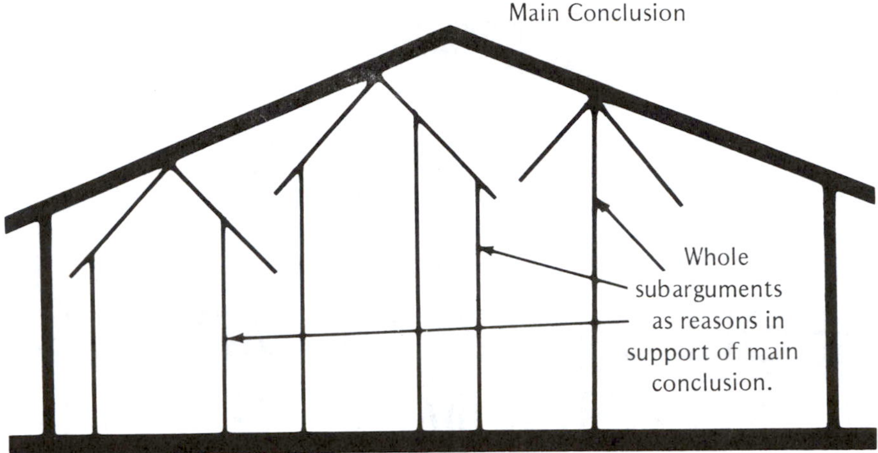

Figure 10.1.

> First of all, the countries have not grown economically. One reason is that they have not been able to achieve a trade surplus, to sell more to other countries than they buy from them. Another reason is that the Latin democracies cannot force their people to export more than they import.
>
> Secondly, the political price of repaying the debt is too high. Inflation is rampant in Brazil. Its effect on the middle class and the poor, who are on fixed incomes, has been devastating. Generals in several countries worry that rampant inflation will benefit groups to the far left or right, which might overthrow these democracies.

Here is a description of this complex argument:

Overall Conclusion: The Latin Democracies cannot repay their debt.
  subconclusion 1 They have not grown economically.
    reason 1 They haven't achieved trade surpluses.
    reason 2 People can't be forced to export more.

  subconclusion 2 The political price of repayment is too high.
    reason 1 Inflation is rampant, causing suffering.
    reason 2 Inflation threatens to destroy the Latin democracies.

The subarguments are the reasons for the main conclusion. The Latin democracies cannot repay their debt because they have not grown economically and because the political price of repayment is too high.

Many complex arguments are not laid out this neatly. Consider the following excerpt from a funny book by one of the world's greatest physicists, the late Richard Feynman:

I *don't* believe I can really do without teaching. The reason is, I have to have something so that when I don't have any ideas and I'm not getting anywhere I can say to myself, "At least I'm living; at least I'm doing something; I'm making some contribution"—it's just psychological.

When I was at Princeton in the 1940's I could see what happened to those great minds at the Institute for Advanced Study, who had been specially selected for their tremendous brains and were now given this opportunity to sit in this lovely house by the woods there, with no classes to teach, with no obligations whatsoever. These poor bastards could now sit and think clearly all by themselves, OK? So they don't get any ideas for a while: They have every opportunity to do something, and they're not getting any ideas. I believe that in a situation like this a kind of guilt or depression worms inside of you, and you begin to *worry* about not getting any ideas. And nothing happens. Still no ideas come.

Nothing happens because there's not enough real activity and challenge: You're not in contact with the experimental guys (the physicists who test out the theories that the theoretical physicists have come up with). You don't have to think how to answer questions from the students. Nothing!

In any thinking process there are moments when everything is going good and you've got wonderful ideas. Teaching is an interruption, and so it's the greatest pain in the neck in the world. And then there are the *longer* periods of time when not much is coming to you. You're not getting any ideas, and if you're doing nothing at all, it drives you nuts! You can't even say "I'm teaching my class."

If you're teaching a class, you can think about the elementary things that you know very well. These things are kind of fun and delightful. It doesn't do any harm to think them over again. Is there a better way to present them? Are there any new problems associated with them? Are there any new thoughts you can make about them? The elementary things are easy to think about; if you can't think of a new thought, no harm done; what you thought about it before is good enough for the class. If you do think of something new, you're rather pleased that you have a new way of looking at it.

The questions of the students are often the source of new research. They often ask profound questions that I've thought about at times and then given up on, so to speak, for a while. It wouldn't do me any harm to think about them again and see if I can go any further now. The students may not be able to see the thing I want to answer, or the subtleties I want to think about, but they *remind* me of a problem by asking questions in the neighborhood of the problem. It's not so easy to remind *yourself* of these things.

So I find that teaching and the students keep life going and I would *never* accept any position in which somebody has invented a happy situation for me where I don't have to teach. Never.[1]

Here is how I saw Feynman's argument, after reading it carefully several times:

Main Conclusion: Feynman needs to teach.

subargument 1 He feels a sense of accomplishment even when he doesn't have any new ideas.

(no reasons offered: it's a loose argument)

subargument 2 Professors without teaching responsibilities become guilty and depressed.
reason: They can't think up new ideas.
"subreason": There's not enough activity and challenge from other students and scientists.

subargument 3 Teaching is good for him.
reason: He can rethink elementary problems.
reason: Students are the source of new research.
"subreason" 1: They often ask profound questions.
"subreason" 2: They remind him of problems he wouldn't think of on his own.

This complex argument even sports some "subreasons," although that term is never used. Can you see why they are dependent on the reason above them?

The final example is an abridged article by mathematician John Allen Paulos. He makes an important argument, and I highly recommend its fuller explanation in his book, *Innumeracy: Mathematical Illiteracy and Its Consequences.*[2]

There are notes on the right-hand side of the text below; cover those notes the first couple of times you read through the argument. Jot down questions and sketch what you believe to be the major argument and its subarguments. Then check your results against the annotations.

The Odds Are You're Innumerate
By John Allen Paulos

Innumeracy, the mathematical analogue of functional illiteracy, afflicts far too many literate people, even widely read and articulate men and women who might cringe if	Would seem to be the main conclusion, but is a subconclusion
words such as "imply" and "infer" were confused. They generally react without a trace of embarrassment, however, to even the most egregious numerical solecisms.	Innumeracy defined; subconclusion: the "highly literate" suffer from it
Once I was at a gathering of writers in which much was being made of the difference between "continually" and "continuously."	Literate people defined
Later that evening, as we were watching the news (another measure of how enjoyable the occasion was), the television meteorologist announced that there was a 50 percent chance of rain for Satur-	Story offered in evidence of how very literate yet very innumerate some people are

day and a 50 percent chance for Sunday as well, and concluded that there was therefore a 100 percent chance of rain that weekend. I grant the mistake was not hilarious, but no one even smiled.

The recent "Mathematics Report Card" released by the Educational Testing Service indicates that more than weather reports are at risk. The rampant innumeracy of our high school students and of the educated public in general is appalling, and since this innumeracy can and does lead to muddled personal decisions, misinformed governmental policies and an increased susceptibility to pseudosciences of all kinds, it's not something that can be easily ignored.

Evidence for high innumeracy rates among high school students

A bigger (the main) conclusion offered here: innumeracy is the cause of large social problems (The odds are that you and many others are innumerate is a subconclusion)

I'm not primarily concerned with esoteric mathematics here, only with some feel for numbers and probabilities, some ability to estimate answers to the ubiquitous questions: How many? How likely? With megaton warheads (equivalent in explosive power to a million tons, or two billions pounds, of TNT) and trillion dollar budgets a reality, people should have a visceral reaction to the difference between a million, a billion and a trillion. (It helps to note that a million seconds takes less than 12 days to tick by, while a billion seconds requires approximately 32 years, and 32,000 years must pass for a trillion seconds to elapse). They needn't be aware of how fast human hair grows, expressed in miles per hour, or of how many basketballs would fit in the Grand Canyon, but they ought to know roughly the population of the United States, the percentage of the world's population that is Chinese, the distance from New York City to Los Angeles, the odds of winning their state lottery and a host of other common magnitudes.

Second definition of numeracy: to estimate numbers and probabilities

Prescription and third definition of numeracy: we should be numerate, defined also as having a gut reaction to difference between a million, billion, and trillion

Distinction between numeracy and concern with trivial mathematical problems

Fourth definition: to know common magnitudes

Without a grasp of such basic numbers, just to cite one example, it is impossible to appreciate the silliness of canceling a European trip because of fear of terrorists. In 1985 when, out of the 28 million Americans who traveled abroad, 17 were killed by terrorists, you were almost 25 times as likely to choke to death (one chance in 68,000), about 300 times as likely to die in a car crash (one chance in 5,300), and nearly

Evidence that many Americans are innumerate: not flying because of terrorist threats

2,000 times as likely to die from the effects of smoking (one chance in 800, the equivalent of three fully loaded jumbo jets crashing each and every day of the year).

Still, what do numbers, probabilities and mathematics in general have to do with books and literature? A couple of minor points first. In addition to the usual reasons for innumeracy, avid readers of fiction sometimes have an extra vulnerability to numerical myopia. Their habit of reading about individuals in extreme and dramatic circumstances may exacerbate the natural tendency we all have to give considerably more weight to unlikely but gripping events than we do to more mundane ones [for example news reports of grisly accidents or killings compared to the many people who successfully lived out the day].

A switch here, back to literate innumerates

Subargument that readers of a lot of fiction are innumerate (give unwarranted weight to likelihood of gripping events)

Reason: they read about extreme situations

. . . Although the numerical imprecisions and distortions associated with fictional (and other) writing may be a trivial matter, they're symptomatic of something much more fundamental. The most obvious causes of innumeracy are poor education and "math anxiety," but the deeper sources are prevailing cultural attitudes, in particular misconceptions about the nature of mathematics. These attitudes and misconceptions lead to an intellectual environment that welcomes and even encourages inadequate mathematical education and pride in ignorance ("I hate math." "Hah. Math was always my worst subject"); they also lead, at least in part, to anxiety when quantitative thinking is required.

The distorted perspective of fictional writing is evidence for the subargument that negative cultural attitudes towards mathematics are the reason for poor math education, pride in ignorance of math, and fear of math

The proverbial disparagement of the English as "a nation of shopkeepers" persists as a belief that a concern with numbers and details numbs one to the big questions, to the grandeur of the natural world. Mathematics is often taken to be mechanical, the work of low-level technicians who will report to the rest of us anything we absolutely must know. Alternatively, mathematics is sometimes thought to have a constraining character that somehow limits our freedom and self-expression.

Subargument
The nature of mathematics is misunderstood because
1. it's thought trivial and
2. a hindrance to big questions
3. it's thought to be mechanical
4. it's thought to limit our freedom

From Wordsworth to present-day New Agers, the romantic idea of communing directly with nature without the distorting aid of any intervening formalisms has also contributed to a vague distaste for mathematics. Sentiments such as these are unfortunately quite prevalent among literary people and ultimately help bring about the abyssmal test scores. . . .

Subargument
Students suffer from innumeracy because literate people [presumably teachers and parents] hold these mistaken views of mathematics

Innumeracy and the attitudes underlying it provide in fact a fertile soil for the growth of pseudoscience. Linda Goodman's "Star Signs" and "Transformation" by Whitley Strieber are simply two of the latest examples of the many books on astrology, numerology, visitations and the like that fill bookstore shelves (annoyingly often in the philosophy sections) and appeal disproportionately to those who have little interest in or knowledge of numbers, probability or basic science.

Evidence for main conclusion: pseudoscience is rampant, as indicated by a number of popular books

Others that attract the same people are Budd Hopkins's "Intruders" and Mr. Strieber's earlier "Communion" (on U.F.O.'s and aliens), the Shirley MacLaine books on reincarnation and psychic communication, J. Z. Knight's "Ramtha" books (on channeling and ancient spirits), George Anderson's conversations with the immortals, New Age books on auras, crystal power and chakras, traditional best sellers like Tarot books and the I Ching, and the collection of volumes on the paranormal that Time-Life Books has recently been hawking on television. Even the Harvard-educated physician and author Michael Crichton, who should know better, claims in his book "Travels" that mentally bending spoons is no big deal, and that virtually everybody at a party he attended was gently rubbing spoons, thereby causing them (bowls too) to flex like rubber. And if many of the diet books, get-rich-quick books, medical fad books and books on how to calculate the appropriate tip in a restaurant are added, one begins to feel it may be a blessing that so few Americans read the books they buy.

Microargument: It's good people don't read books they buy because they buy so much junk!

In "Pseudoscience and Society in Nineteenth-Century America," Arthur Wrobel remarks that belief in phrenology,* homeopathy** and hydropathy*** was not confined to the poor and the ignorant, but pervaded much of 19th-century literature. Such credulity is not as extensive in contemporary literature, but astrology is one pseudoscience that does seem to engage a big segment of the reading public. Literary allusions to it abound. . . . A 1986 Gallup poll showed that 52 percent of American teen-agers subscribe to it. . . .

Historical claim, that pseudoscience was popular among the literate in the 19th century

Given these figures, it may not be entirely inappropriate to note here that no mechanism through which the alleged zodiacal influences exert themselves has ever been specified by astrologers. Gravity certainly cannot account for these natal influences, since even the gravitational pull of the attending obstetrician is orders of magnitude greater than that of the relevant planet or planets. Nor is there any empirical evidence; top astrologers (as determined by their peers) have failed repeatedly to associate personality profiles with astrological data at a rate higher than that of chance. Neither of these fatal objections to astrology, of course, is likely to carry much weight with literate but innumerate people who don't estimate magnitudes or probabilities, or who are overimpressed by vague coincidences yet unmoved by overwhelming statistical evidence.

Subargument
Astrology is not credible because:
1. No mechanism (model) is offered to explain it (See chapter 12 for a discussion of models).
2. Gravity cannot explain astrology.
3. No astrologers have been able to do better than random at guessing at personality on the basis of star signs

Arrayed against fatuous books on stars, the mind and numbers are some excellent expository works on the same topics. These include, among many others, "A Brief History of Time" by Stephen Hawking, Rudy Rucker's "Mind Tools," Martin Gardner's many books and essays, James Gleick's "Chaos," "The Blind Watchmaker" by Richard Dawkins, "The Cosmic Code" by Heinz Pagels, Timothy Ferris's "Coming of Age in the Milky Way," Stephen Jay Gould's books, Douglas Hofstadter's "Gödel, Escher, Bach," Carl Sagan's "Cosmos," "The Loss of Certainty" by Morris Kline, "The Mathematical Experience" by Philip Davis and Reu-

Prescription to read these books instead

*predicting character traits by the size of bumps on various places on the head

**use of minute amounts of a disease-causing substance (for instance, bacteria) to cure that disease

***the use of water as a cure

ben Hersh. With a few exceptions, however, such books don't reach a big readership and, because they are difficult, they preach to the converted and inform the informed.

In regard to mathematics at least, something more is needed—books, articles and columns that address a much larger audience and deal not so much with the subject proper as with critical appraisals of the way it is applied and of the misunderstandings and confusions that arise naturally from these applications. Such writings would not change cultural attitudes towards mathematics, of course, but by making its effects concrete and by relating it to matters that are important to all of us, they might help significantly. An overlooked, yet natural, forum for these discussions is the daily newspapers and the general circulation magazines. (If they can carry regular horoscopes, why not entertainingly written articles on the consequences of number numbness?). . . .

Prescription to educate the public to innumeracy problems through daily newspapers and magazines

Microargument: They should carry articles on innumeracy because they carry regular horoscopes

It is distressing that a society and culture that depend so critically on mathematics and its uses should nevertheless seem so indifferent to the innumeracy and general mathematical ignorance of even its brightest citizens. Gauss* will never touch us the way Flaubert** does, but people should at least recognize his name.[3]

"Loose" prescription: People should know who Gauss was

SUMMARY

A complex argument has the same features as a simple one; but it is a larger structure containing subarguments whose conclusions usually function as reasons in support of the major conclusion.

EXERCISES

1. Diagram and analyze the reading "The Case for Limited Animal Rights" at the end of this chapter.
2. Diagram and analyze the excerpt from "Gossip," at the end of chapter 8.

*Carl Friedrich Gauss (1777–1855), one of the world's greatest mathematicians.

**Gustave Flaubert, one of the world's greatest novelists, who lived in the 19th century.

3. Construct a complex argument about the death penalty, then diagram it. (Remember, a complex argument does not consist of one argument for and one argument against a position; it is an argument with a main conclusion supported by smaller, strict arguments.)

READING

Challenged by Singer's argument for animal rights (chapter 2), I set out to construct an alternative position, which became this complex argument. In light of my argument, can you think of ways to strengthen Singer's—and vice versa?

The Case for Limited Animal Rights

The question of what rights animals should enjoy is a vexatious one, involving a Gordian knot of ancillary issues. The problem, too, is not without significance, because hundreds of millions of animals are put to death for human use each year.* About four hundred animal rights groups have been mounting publicity campaigns which range from appeals for increased restrictions on scientific experimentation and animal farming to the admonition of strict vegetarianism and discontinuance of all animal experiments. These groups have as their end the prevention of what they perceive to be needless suffering of helpless victims. Were it clear what "needless suffering" means, and were there no serious ramifications to the imposition of further restraints on scientific research and animal husbandry, the solutions would be clear. But there are problems.

It is not well appreciated, for example, that slowing down scientific research would retard discovery of antidotes to diseases such as cancer which kill humans and animals alike. Given the bureaucratic snarl in England that has resulted from overseeing "animal handlers," it is certainly unrealistic to expect that regulation would not have a slowing effect. Thus, many thousands more people and animals would die through delays in research than would have died if a few thousand animals had been put to death in the course of discovering an antidote. Furthermore, the benefits to the many at the expense of the few are even more impressive if one calculates future years. The death, say, of 500,000 animals in the course of cancer research will make possible the prolongation of the lives of many millions of animals and people into the foreseeable future. Ironically, it may be the very success of hard-won discoveries in warding off disease that makes this trade-off difficult for animal rights advocates to appreciate. Yet as recently as the 1930s, deformity, pain, and disability were far more common, even in the developed countries. A partial listing of vaccines acquired through animal research which have saved millions of animals' lives would include anthrax, distemper, typhoid, cholera, plague, and recently, feline leukemia.

The list for humans would include polio and measles vaccines, antibiotics, immunizations for diphtheria, smallpox, dramatic strides in surgical techniques, and treatments for cancer. Even current knowledge of effective

*Of course, humans are animals too. But to avoid the cumbersome phrase "nonhuman animals," the term "animals" in the rest of this essay will refer to nonhuman animals, with the distinction understood to be an artificial one.

hygiene and good nutrition is in large part the result of animal experimentation. But many health problems are still unsolved: chronic neurological disease, schizophrenia, senile dementia, most forms of cancer, deafness, blindness, arthritis, and autoimmune diseases. Without animal experimentation, there will be no end to these diseases.[4]

Of course, a catalog of advantages does not end the discussion. A counterargument could be raised that these comparatively few experimental animals are killed or made to suffer without their consent; so the end of prolonging the lives of many does not justify employing the means of deliberately hurting the nonconsenting few.

This counterargument contains two important assumptions: that animal life is as important as human life, and that animals have absolute rights to life and freedom from suffering. But these principles, if applied in all interactions between humans and animals, would lead to monstrous results in daily life. A minor infestation of house mice would, unchecked, spread across an entire city, mice and their droppings creating great health hazards. To respond that cats could be brought in to kill the mice is odd, since if animals have absolute rights to life, then cats would have no more right to kill mice than humans (and surely humans would be "accessories after the fact" in putting cats up to it). This brings to light another problem: What will animals eat if all animals have rights to life? If animal life is as important as human life, do humans have a moral obligation to try to put all animals in the world, wild and domestic, on a vegetarian diet? Even if one counters that animals are entitled to kill other animals because it is their instinct, while humans should be above killing animals under any circumstances, the problem of overpopulation by rodents or other animals remains, as does the problem of feeding pets. It would be cruel to turn out domesticated pets to forage for themselves. Many millions would die in fights with others or from lack of food. It therefore seems wise, for the sake of animals as much as humans, to retreat from the extreme view that all animals have an absolute right to life. Most people would also shrink from the practical implications of the conclusion that animal life is as important as human, since such implications would entail more animal and human misery than now exists.

But that is not to say that animals should have no rights whatever. Currently, legislation exists in all states to protect animals from senseless abuse. There are sanctions against tormenting an animal with no other object in mind. The question now being raised, however, is whether this is enough. Proponents of animal rights, such as Peter Singer, have answered in the negative, doing much to remind us that even when using animals for other ends than just to be cruel, we are still using sentient beings, perhaps as capable as we of feeling pain. For the most part, activists' concern is limited to mammals because of the similarity of their nervous systems to that of humans. (Reptiles and so-called lower forms of life are not at issue, thus raising the specter of future accusations of "mammalism"—that mammals have been unjustly singled out over, say, arachnids and plants as worthy of concern.)

Staying with those animals who have offered evidence of an ability to suffer, such an ability would seem to count as important for reasons of fellow feeling. Were I a mouse about to be killed, I would far rather die painlessly than in agony. An argument might therefore be made on the basis of compassion that a homeowner should use mouse traps rather than poison, supposing that the former is less painful for the mouse. (Trapping a house mouse and releasing it in the backyard or nearby hills will not rid that area of the problem, but pass on the need to kill to someone else. Or is it incumbent on the homeowner to make a trip far out of town with the mouse?) It is thus not hard to argue that animals, be they house mice or deer, should be dispatched as painlessly as possible if they are so numerous that they would starve. The point here too is that for reasons of animal or human well-being, mice, deer, or any animals not facing species extinction,* should forfeit their lives.

The assumptions beneath this argument have been, of course, that humans are more important than animals, and humans may kill animals under certain circumstances. Thus baldly put, these attitudes bother people who recollect a worldwide history of cruelty and prejudice by humans against other humans. Isn't the assertion that humans are more important than animals yet one more instance of chauvinism?

Cases of prejudice against other humans are not analogous to the issue at hand. No other species has the ability to be the steward of the planet's animals. And since a great deal of human and animal misery would result if humans were to abdicate this stewardship, they should retain it. Further, humans can't share the job of animal-management with animals. Humans can, however, share such jobs as choosing leaders and formulating guidelines for animal experimentation with other humans. The very absurdity of extending equality of opportunity for jobs, the vote, and animal-management to animals points to the vast difference in these situations. (An interesting note is that although humans have often behaved badly towards animals, even driving some species into extinction, no other species has demonstrated the altruism which mankind has in fostering other species. Were another species intelligent enough to actually participate in decision-making about other animals, it is not clear that its members would show other than the narrowest self-interest.)

But difficult questions remain. Even though animals don't share equal status with humans, is it justifiable to inflict pain on them? In cases of scientific research, and given the argument of the greater importance of the many, the answer should be yes. Yet out of respect for fellow sentient beings, experiments should be performed only under these conditions: that there is no good alternative procedure; that good science is being done; that no experiment already performed is needlessly repeated; that any experiment should be conducted with the least possible infliction of suffering; that there be open scrutiny of the experiment and its results among the community of scientists. These standards should be prerequisites for all experiments. But how often are they honored, and who should enforce them in their breach?

In fact, severe pain is very rare in animal experimentation, partly because scientists are as humane as anyone else, partly because severe pain would kill the animal or otherwise destroy the experiment through the physiological disturbances it causes. Animals are anesthetized for more severe invasions and then killed. The most the average laboratory animal feels is the passing discomfort of a shot. Of course, the ideal would be to develop technologically to the point of using cells instead of animals, but for

*A distinction can be made in cases of endangered species on the grounds that their very uniqueness gives their lives greater weight against larger numbers of nonendangered species, including human, because although humans are more important, all species are *close* enough in worth to merit their survival.

the moment animals are required in a great many cases. Such technological transcendence of animals might be achieved, but ironically, only after more animal experimentation reveals how to do so.

On the premise that no one is better able to judge the value of a research proposal than a scientist's colleagues in the area in question, scientists should continue to judge whether an investigator's proposal is worthy of funding; in so doing, they will also continue to judge whether the animal research involved is appropriate. Were someone outside the field of expertise to have power to halt research, many important, lifesaving projects would suffer because of ignorance.

As an additional safeguard for animals, many universities have set up animal boards, consisting of several licensed veterinarians. The scientific investigators submit their research proposals to the boards each year. More safeguards might be built with the formulation of ethical guidelines for scientists, as well as the creation of required short courses in which more experienced researchers pass on practical advice to less experienced colleagues. For example, an inexperienced researcher might struggle with guinea pigs as he tried to decapitate them. A more experienced researcher could point out that the guinea pigs might be made unconscious with carbon dioxide, then killed, thus ensuring that they wouldn't suffer.

Basically, what is now being done within the scientific community involves the warranted and nonabusive use of animals. Moreover, it is important to remember that of all the animals put to human use each year, a very small percentage are used in scientific research—most are eaten.

It would seem that a movement to forbid any work on animals, thus permitting the death of many more animals and people, reflects a prejudice against laboratory experiments as in themselves horrifying incarnations of evil. Or it may reflect a desire for absolute moral perfection, even painlessness, in a world that is full of pain and whose biological basis depends largely on killing to eat. And even now, despite the many medical breakthroughs, there remains much pain. It is odd that the comparatively minimal animal suffering which carries the hope of reducing immense amounts of future suffering should be so bitterly attacked.

The case against permitting animals raised for food to suffer is harder to counter, because here the infliction of discomfort does not result in a diminution of it somewhere else. Furthermore, humans can, with some effort, be perfectly well nourished without eating animals. So animals are raised for bringing additional pleasure and variety to the human diet, rather than to forestall future suffering, as in scientific experiments. If it is true that hundreds of millions of factory farm animals are, every moment of the day, denied such elementary freedoms as the space to walk a few steps or stretch their limbs, that seems unwarranted cruelty to sentient beings. Learning that pigs and chickens are frequently raised in such close quarters that they cannot turn around, and that this is done solely for finanical reasons, is disturbing. Farmers may need to strike agreements with one another to undertake the expense of providing more room in which to raise animals. Or perhaps legislation is needed. The results would be higher production costs and the passing on of higher prices for humane animal husbandry to the public, but an informed and understanding public should be willing to pay the price. To the argument that animals should not be raised for food at all, one might counter that the animal farmer is the domestic animal's best friend, since it is only because of the farmer—and his client, the meat-eater—

that so many cows, chickens, and pigs have had the privilege of living at all. The question, however, is whether the farm animal, pen-raised for slaughter, is better off for having lived. If conditions under which the animals are raised are humane, the answer would seem to be affirmative.

A sticky, middle issue is research conducted for the consumer. It is in between the foregoing issues in this sense: Like food-animals, new products bring pleasure to humans; but as with scientific research, failure to experiment with animals could result in the injury of many unsuspecting humans. So for the sake of the consumer, millions of animals are sacrificed each year to meet the public demand for safety—not to advance science, but to make sure that substitutes for sugar will not cause cancer, or that mouthwashes will not irritate the skin. Since myriad such consumer products now exist, one might well ask why the chance must be taken of inflicting pain on animals merely to give the world a product such as a new after-shave lotion.

Experiments for consumer products should be carefully distinguished from scientific experiments. Humans choose new consumer products. They do not choose to get neurological diseases. Further, consumer products are for pleasure; products of scientific research are for the prolongation of life. Perhaps, then, humans should bear the risk of using caustic products-for-pleasure, rather than subjecting animals to it. But the public might not approve of the implications of this solution. No company would be willing to take the financial risks involved in developing new products unless those burned could not readily sue a company that put untested products on the market (or not collect the huge damage awards now granted). Yet the ability to sue for injury from a product up to now has been a far more sacred cow in this country than the regard in which experimental animals have been held. It will be interesting indeed if animal rights activists can change these priorities.

In sum, not one but three quite different situations exist which demand consideration of animals' rights. In cases of future betterment of animals and humans through scientific experiment, animals may be made to suffer, but the minimum amount necessary. Animals bred and raised for food should be better off alive than if they had never been born. And since human use of a number of products is only for pleasure, yet testing these products involves pain to animals, humans should be willing to knowingly bear these risks. Beneath all three conclusions lie the principles that animals are not as important as humans but should not suffer unless that suffering might forestall future unavoidable suffering of other animals and humans.

Even though the aforementioned solutions seem better than the alternatives, are they truly fair to animals? What if superintelligent beings from Alpha Centauri landed on earth and decided to use *us* for their experiments, arguing that they could save far more of our, and their, lives by so doing? Would the same arguments apply against humans as have been used to give animals fewer rights? If our intelligence were at all within the realm of theirs, then the foregoing argument that we should share decision-making and exemption from experimentation could apply. But what if they countered that their intelligence was so exquisitely refined compared with ours (say as ours is to that of mice) that we couldn't even begin to help them in their stewardship of the galaxy? Would that entitle them to raise us (humanely) for food and use us (as painlessly as possible, but occasionally in pain) for the betterment of our life spans and the lives of others in the galaxy? Let us hope that such advanced beings would have the technological ability to transcend the need for experimental animals.

NOTES

[1]Reprinted from *"Surely You're Joking, Mr. Feynman!" The Adventures of a Curious Character*, Richard P. Feynman, as told to Ralph Leighton, edited by Edward Hutchings, pp. 165–166, by permission of W. W. Norton & Company, Inc. Copyright © 1985 by Richard P. Feynman and Ralph Leighton.

[2]John Allen Paulos, *Innumeracy: Mathematical Illiteracy and Its Consequences* (New York: Hill and Wang, a division of Farrar, Straus and Giroux, 1988).

[3]John Allen Paulos, "The Odds Are You're Innumerate," *The New York Times Book Review*, January 1, 1989. Copyright © 1989 by The New York Times Company. Reprinted by permission.

[4]See William Paton, *Man and Mouse: Animals in Medical Research* (New York: Oxford University Press, 1984), pp. 45–72.

CHAPTER ELEVEN

DELIBERATIONS

ARE DELIBERATIONS BETTER THAN DEBATES?

This is a chapter on how to "un-debate."

The trouble with debates is that the participants so rarely seek the truth—each is seeking to win, and in attempting to win, it is all too easy to bend the truth. Furthermore, in a debate it is a mark of failure to concede that the other side is right.*

Another objection to debates is their bruising quality. We've probably all been shellacked by somebody whose only merit was to be more persistently obtuse than we were at driving home a point. Unless one suffers from sadomasochistic tendencies, therefore, it is best to avoid debates.

Here Both Sides Win

On the other hand, we need to interact as members of the community of thinkers. The stance of the balanced critical thinker is, as Karl Popper

*In *The Republic,* the ancient Greek philosopher Plato warned against the trap of being one who "when he thinks that he is reasoning . . . is only disputing . . . and he will pursue a merely verbal opposition in the spirit of contention and not of fair discussion."

put it, "I may be wrong and you may be right, and by an effort, we may get nearer to the truth."

To work this idea out practically, you can use a scheme which is a cross between a debate and a discussion.

Two or more people start out on opposite sides of an issue, but for the purpose of consulting with one another to reach a decision. They argue as persuasively as possible at the beginning, but then they really listen to the other side(s) and decide whether to change course. They are deliberating over an issue, not debating with one another. It's fine if by the end they've decided to stay on the same side of the issue that they began on; it's fine if both end on one side; it's perfectly fine if they end up having switched positions. The emphasis here is on *getting at the truth* as best one sees it.

Play the Devil's Advocate

Everyone should play the devil's advocate from time to time. This means to counterargue some position that is put forward, not because you necessarily believe your counterargument (you probably don't), but for the fun and enlightenment of seeing where this argument will take you. Again, you don't hang on to the death, but try to take this counterargument towards the truth of the matter. Here is some language to get you into the game:

Let me play the devil's advocate and argue that . . .
One could make the argument that . . .
A case could be made that . . .

If you hit upon an idea and want to try it out, playing the devil's advocate in the middle of a deliberation is perfectly acceptable.

Formal Deliberations

The more you deliberate and play the devil's advocate with others, the more quickly you'll become skilled in critical thinking. Make arrangements to meet fellow classmates to practice, or train some loved one in the sport.

You might also want to hold formal deliberations in class. Here is one possible system of points. The numbers represent the maximum possible points you can receive for each category.

POINTS FOR

20 points for using critical thinkers' language and twelve tools of argumentation during the deliberation.
20 points for producing a cogent, well-supported opening argument.

5 points each time you request a definition of a pivotal term or make a distinction.
10 points for trying to harmonize the other side's claims with your point of view. It may work or it may not, but the idea is to try.
10 points for playing the devil's advocate.

Then points for one of the following:

20 points for changing your position if you give an argument why you're changing that takes the other side into account (e.g., explain the specific point or points the opposite side has that seem true and can't be taken into account by your argument).

or

20 points for not changing your position if you give an argument why you're not changing that takes the other side into account (e.g., "despite the other argument that," or " 'even granting' the argument, my argument still holds, because").

That makes a total of 75 points (more if you request more definitions or distinctions as often as the deliberation genuinely needs them).

POINTS OFF

20 points off for being sarcastic or otherwise uncivil (distinguish "sarcasm" and "incivility" to one's partner from showing frustration at not getting one's point across).

Whatever Is Right

As in a debate, you are rewarded for coming up with strongly supported arguments. If you believe it is right to maintain your original position, you are rewarded as long as you show you've considered the other side. Unlike in a debate, however, if you start to become convinced by the other side you are rewarded for being flexible and altering your position.

An Example

This should give you a flavor of how a deliberation might go. Because the participants are arguing on their feet, you can't expect the close rigor of a written dialogue, nor even that of a written argument, unless those participating are very skilled. The language and tools of this deliberation over which method of verbal argument is better (debate or deliberation?) are in boldface. First, Jennifer presents her *prepared remarks:*

I will argue that debates are a much better way to argue than deliberations. **By definition,** debaters are supposed to argue their sides right to the end. **That implies that** they're going to argue just as hard as they can. With a deliberation, **on the other hand,*** it is too easy to give up on your side earlier than you should. If you can get as many points for "caving in" as you can for pushing your point, why go to the trouble?

As evidence to support my claim that debates are the best way to argue, the debating style is used in all crucial arguments: In life-and-death matters, attorneys debate in courts of law; in deciding the future leader of our country, we have the presidential aspirants debate; in determining whether to vote a bill into law, Congress debates its pros and cons. Just because somebody gets his or her feelings hurt once in a while **is no reason** to eliminate this valuable means of getting at the truth.

Mike then presents his prepared remarks:

My argument is that deliberating is the best way to argue. So often in a debate the flashiest argument is the one that wins. It often happens that in a debate the arguers get backed into maintaining positions that they don't even believe, just to save face or to try to win the argument. With a deliberation, **on the other hand,** there are no "winners" or "losers," just two people working together to decide on the likeliest conclusion of an issue.

I would further argue that debates have harmed the cause of argument rather than helped it. **In support of this claim,** I ask you to consider how rarely you and the people you know want to get into "arguments" about topics that they care a great deal about, because argument in their minds implies a painful debating session.

Getting at the truth is much more important than winning, and **on this assumption I base my argument that** deliberations are the best choice for argument.

Jennifer's and Mike's *extemporaneous remarks* follow (look for critical thinking language and counterarguing strategies):

JENNIFER: I'd like a definition of "flashiest arguments."
MIKE: Um . . . they are the ones where people are more dramatic or forceful.
JENNIFER: O.K., but haven't you created a false dichotomy? I mean, couldn't somebody be very dramatic and right?
MIKE: Yes, they could, but my point is that in trying so hard to be dramatic and to win the debate, they can easily lose track of being right. I mean, haven't you gotten into a debate with your mom or

*points out a distinction

dad about staying out late at night, and because you've wanted to so badly you've said things that even you don't believe?
JENNIFER: Yes, but would a deliberation really solve that problem? I mean, since I want to stay out so badly, how is a deliberation going to make it less of a scene?
MIKE: Well, if you go with the attitude of figuring out the best course of action and argue your case as hard as you can at the beginning, I'd still count that a deliberation.
JENNIFER: What do you mean by "at the beginning"?
MIKE: That's a tough one to call. I'd say that it's when the sides both pretty much understand each other. Then it's time to really look at what the other side has said and consider it.
JENNIFER: Don't you think people would look like fools if they changed their minds in the middle of an argument? What if it's a presidential debate and the Democrat suddenly says, "Oh, I see you've been right all along, I'm going to go out and register Republican."
MIKE: I see your point. We've come to expect political candidates and leaders not to change their minds, which is weird. Why should *we* get to change our minds and they don't get to change theirs?
JENNIFER: Well, they say they're going to do a thing, and we vote for them because they're going to do it.
MIKE: Maybe that's the problem. Maybe we should just accept a candidate's assumptions and . . . I mean, accept one candidate's assumptions as better than the other's and vote for her on that basis. Then if she changes her mind, that's O.K.
JENNIFER: [a bit impatient]: Look, you can't hope to change the world. It's just a fact that most people vote for a candidate on the basis of how strong a leader he is. If he can't decide what to do and shows that in a debate, I don't think he should be in office.
MIKE: Well, I'll agree with you that it would take a long time for people to expect deliberations rather than debates out of candidates. Let's accept that that won't happen soon. But what about our daily lives? I think that we don't talk about the things that really matter to us because we don't want to get into a debate over these issues.
JENNIFER: I don't think that's why we don't talk about these things. It's because we're afraid of being wrong and having to change. If I believe that abortion is right and suddenly am confronted with some ideas that throw this into question, then I'm not going to be comfortable. It has nothing to do with whether I have a deliberation to find out these uncomfortable ideas or if it's a debate.
MIKE: I'll grant you that all types of arguments can turn up some uncomfortable ideas. Aren't we missing a central piece of evidence? We don't know whether people would be more willing to deliberate

than debate. Would you be willing to try an experiment? We could poll whatever number of people you think would make a convincing sample to at least see what people *think* they'd prefer.
JENNIFER: Or how about just trying both methods out on a group of people?
MIKE: That's O.K. with me too. (slyly) You know, Jennifer, you worked this deliberation out very well.
JENNIFER: Heck, no! This was a debate!

SUMMARY

A deliberation is a form of discussion in which two people begin on different sides of an issue. Each person argues his or her position with the best, most truthful means possible. Then each decides, in light of the other argument, whether to adopt the other position, to change his or her position somewhat, or to maintain the same position. Both sides realize that to modify one's position is not to lose; the point is to get closer to the truth of the matter.

EXERCISE

Get a classmate, family member, or friend to deliberate with you on any issue of mutual interest.

CHAPTER TWELVE

EXPERIMENT, CORRELATION, AND SPECULATION

Experiment, correlation, and speculation—your appreciation of how these types of evidence differ will greatly enhance your critical acumen. This chapter elaborates upon the information presented in chapter 4.

It's best to grant *any* argument only provisional status pending a better argument, no matter what the nature of the evidence. You will often find a critical thinker's favorable assessment of an argument in such terms as **"the best argument on this subject to date."** The rule of faith here is that a better argument, theory, or hypothesis may appear on any subject, thanks to the community of thinkers.

Experimental evidence is frequently used in science to get at underlying mechanisms in the material world. Experimental evidence is gathered in the social and behavioral sciences too, whenever possible and whenever doing so would not endanger the subjects' well-being. In cases where experimental evidence can't be obtained, correlation or evidence gathered after the fact is used. Finally, evidence based on reason and shared experience is speculative. Following are more detailed examinations of each type of evidence.

EXPERIMENT

One of the most important aspects of knowing about anything is to know what caused it.

Until recently in human history, people were stuck with trying to understand how things were caused by just looking at some situation and fishing for cause-effect connections.

They would see W happen, and then Y would happen. They would infer that W had caused Y. The argument is "because W (reason), therefore Y (conclusion)."

Some of the beliefs arrived at in this fashion now strike us as weird or unfair; for example, the notion that applying leeches and bleeding people would cure fevers, or that witches could make others do evil. Those who believed these causal connections were quite intelligent, presumably just as intelligent as we are. But the problem they faced was that there are usually many more factors than just a W and a Y in a situation. There are all sorts of other events.

As the arrows in Figure 12.1 indicate, each object is acting or moving in a different way. There are many possible causes for any given event (Y), be it a poorly running car, increased hormonal activity, or anything else. The problem is how to sort out those factors that don't matter and find the cause of Y's motion or behavior. Scientific method has given us a way to deal with this problem and gain good evidence for cause and effect.

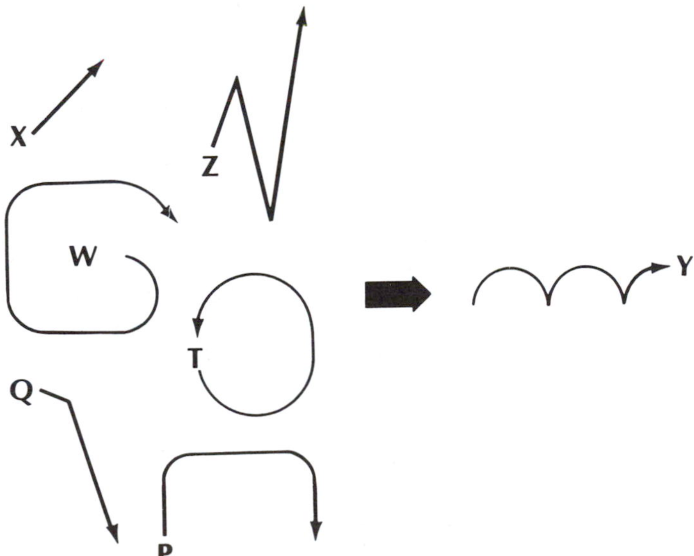

Figure 12.1. Which of these moving objects is the cause of Y's motion?

There are two sides to the methodology of science. The first is that of model-building. The second is that of experimental setup.

Model-building

Although we may have identified causal factors, we don't yet necessarily know the mechanism whereby X causes Y to move. With a combination of careful yet creative thinking, the scientist gets an idea about the way that some process might work. That idea, or model (also called hypothesis, or theory), outstrips the available evidence. The model should also obey two rules:

Rule 1: It should be the *simplest explanation* of the expected evidence. (Another way of stating this is that, given a choice between two theories which explain some evidence, the simpler theory would be superior.) This principle was first enunciated by William of Ockham in the twelfth century, and is known as Ockham's razor. The simplest plausible hypothesis is better, since it is much easier to work with.

Rule 2: The model should have *high predictive power*. It should help us to see many other connections: "If this is the case, then X and Y and Z facts should be found in the future."

Once we have a theory, we can test its predictions with the experimental setup.

An Example

Model-building to get at causation is not the same as speculation. The scientific origin of the atomic theory, that is, the idea that everything is made up of atoms, began with the work of John Dalton, Joseph Louis Gay-Lussac, and Amedeo Avogadro. This idea was actually speculated upon by the ancient Greek philosophers. They debated the question whether tiny, invisible particles might compose all matter. However, they had a serious objection: How could the complexity of nature be explained by atoms, which they believed differed only slightly from one another? That is, how could living things, rocks, and air be made of the same components? Unfortunately, these ideas of the Greeks lacked the essential feature of a scientific theory: They were not supported or tested by experiments. These ideas were not tested against the realities of the world. Since they were the product of conjecture, they could be demolished by more conjecture.

Two thousand years after the Greeks' atomic speculations, Dalton formulated the first atomic theory. The scientists of that time had found that chemical compounds, regardless of their source, were always made up of the same ratios of the same elements; for example, that mercuric oxide was always made up of a certain proportion of mercury for a certain amount of oxygen (for instance, say, 200 grams of mercury always combined with 16 grams of oxygen). No matter how much mercuric oxide scientists decomposed, they always found the two components, mercury and oxygen, in the same proportion (Fig. 12.2).

Then they realized that the same components could be joined in different proportions and yield quite different chemicals. "Different" here means different smells, color, etc. For example, three combinations of nitrogen and oxygen were known, each with different properties. At zero degrees two of these chemicals are colorless gases; the third is a yellow liquid. Furthermore, at very low temperatures one of the gases becomes a colorless liquid, the other a blue liquid. Each combination was made up of different ratios of oxygen and nitrogen (e.g., one is 14 g of nitrogen with 16 g of oxygen; another is 14 g of nitrogen, 32 g of oxygen; the third is 28 g of nitrogen and 16 g of oxygen) (Fig. 12.3).

A simple explanation for these and other findings was that the elements (oxygen, nitrogen, etc.) were made up of *atoms*, basic particles which could combine in different ratios to yield *molecules* with different properties. This is the beginning of atomic theory. So the model that everything is made up of atoms explains how we can have such a diversity of compounds. This, of course, got around the problems the Greeks had about the multiplicity of things they saw. Furthermore, the atomic theory gave rise to many successful and important predictions which comprise modern chemistry. One of the most dramatic examples that comes to mind

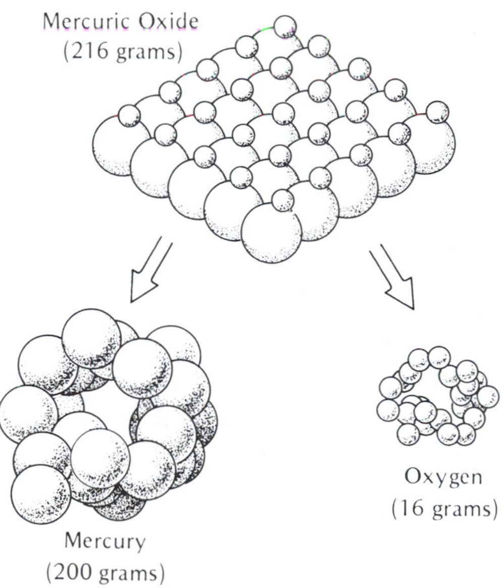

Figure 12.2

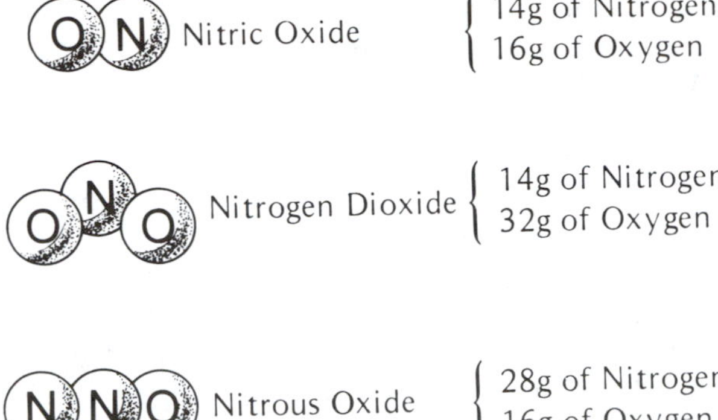

Figure 12.3

is the probing of the structure of the atom which eventually led to the ability to release atomic energy.

All of the foregoing exactitude about the ratio of grams in mercuric oxide is data upon which scientific model-building depends. Early chemists obtained these data by using the experimental setup.

The Experimental Setup

Rather than just looking at one situation and trying to fish out a cause from any number of candidates, the procedure here is to take one possibility at a time. Taking the example shown in Figure 12.1, we systematically go through and allow only *one* of these factors to operate at a time and see whether Y moves or not.

The factors (letters on the left) are not allowed to move. Only x is permitted to move (Fig. 12.4). This is the experimental situation. One of two things is going to happen here. Either Y will move or it won't. Say that Y doesn't move. Then we can rule out the possibility that X caused Y to move. But suppose that Y does move. Even if Y does move, we *still* can't be

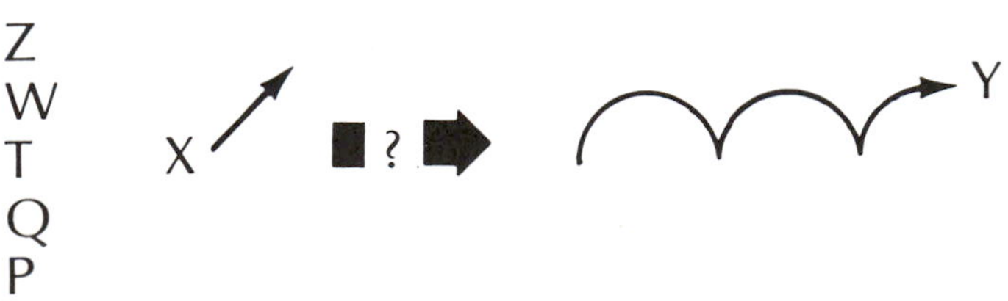

Figure 12.4

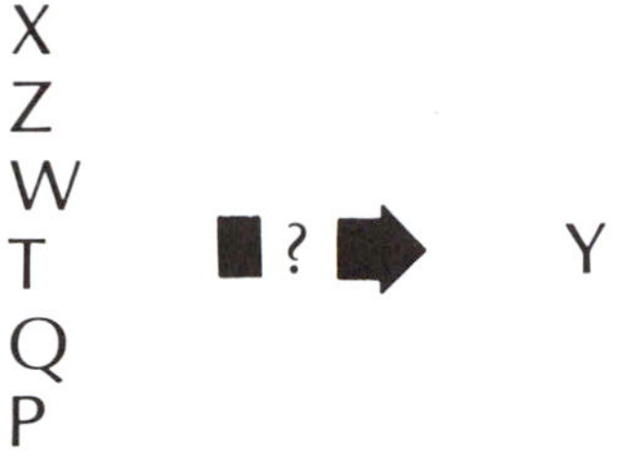

Figure 12.5

sure that X is the cause until we hold X (and all the others, Z, W, T, Q, P, etc.) motionless and see that Y in fact does *not* move under those circumstances. We have to be sure that Y moves only when X does.

As Figure 12.5 shows, an almost identical situation, called *the control*, is set up. The only difference between the experimental and the control situation is that in this latter case everything is held down, including Y. Now if Y doesn't "perform," we can conclude that X is the cause. In effect, when X is in play, Y is affected (experiment). When X is out of play, Y is not affected (control).

The scientist can proceed to systematically try each variable (Z,W,T, Q,P) in the same way as X, always comparing that result with the control situation. We always want to be assured that when a factor is out of commission the effect is, too.

Experiment-Control at Work

Let's consider two examples of the experimental method, since this duality of experimental and control systems is part of every scientific experiment. To take a simple example, say we want to test for the ability of blood to catalyze (carry out) a chemical reaction, transforming compound A into compound B. If we want to find out whether blood could carry out this transformation, we would mix compound A with some blood, wait several minutes, and then look for the presence of B. But even if we found B, we would need to do the control experiment, mixing A with water to see how much, if any, B accumulated after the same period. Why would we have to do the control experiment? We want to be certain that it is the *blood*, and not some property in A itself, that is causing the change (see Fig. 12.6).

As a second example from a different scientific area, consider the extraction of oil from oil shale. Engineers are constantly testing new methods against old methods of extraction, the new methods being the experimental methods, the old functioning as the control. They extract many samples with both methods and compare the results. Small differences in

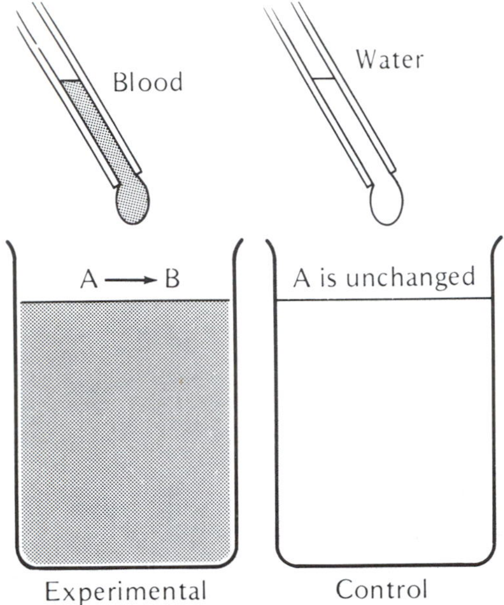

Figure 12.6

the two methods carried out with large amounts of material make enormous differences in terms of cost or amount of oil obtained or pollution generated, among other things.

This tactic of discovering causes by means of two systems (experimental and control) has to be one of the greatest discoveries in history. It has literally put us on a rocket ship, compared with the slow walk of former times to gather strong evidence.

Improving Models, Improving Experiments

The model and consequent experiment don't exist in isolation. They are part of an ongoing building project. Think of a constant cycle by which our understanding improves through thousands of orbits from model to experiments to model (Fig. 12.7). The theory gives rise to predictions. These predictions are used to design the experiments, which test the predictions. The new experimental data that is generated will cause the model to be accepted, rejected, or—what is usually the case—modified to better fit the data.

This cycle has given birth to an enormous number of refined, related offspring in physics, chemistry, and biology. When a sufficient amount and complexity of powerful evidence exist, a separate discipline emerges. In engineering, for instance, chemical engineering, structural engineering, and, recently, genetic engineering are the practical application of scientifically derived theories.

The existence of an elaborate engineering—this power to manipulate

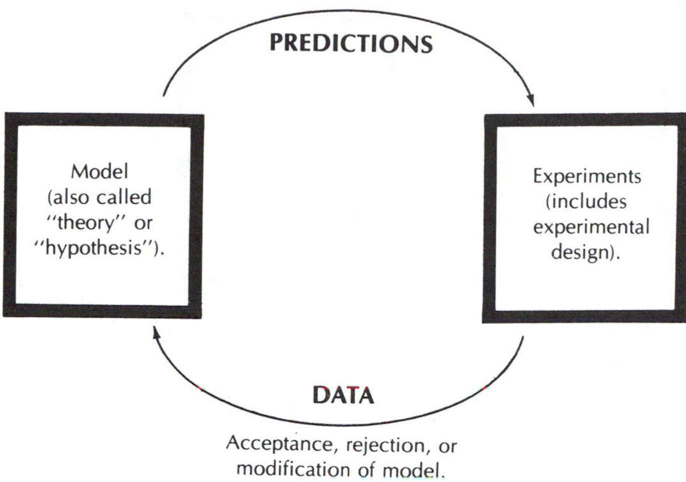

Figure 12.7

the phenomenon in very intricate ways—is good evidence that the models in a particular scentific area correspond with what's "out there" in the world.

The Cycle at Work

A model can be abstract and represented in mathematical terms. Or it can actually take the shape of a structure, much as a plastic airplane model is a miniaturized image. Let's take the example of the genetic material, DNA. The scientists who determined its structure had originally expressed their hypothesis in the form of a physical model. Of course, unlike an airplane model, this model was more than a million times *larger* than the original.

Experiments before 1953 showed that DNA could give bacteria new genetic traits. Thus it appeared to be the material that stores the information of inheritance. In 1953, James Watson and Francis Crick proposed a model for the structure of the molecule DNA. Figure 12.8 shows the operation of the cycle. The experiments focused scientists' attention on the possibility that DNA stores genetic information.

First, this new model for the structure of the DNA molecule explained the well-known rules of inheritance, such as that a woman has an almost equal chance of having a boy or girl baby. Furthermore, it predicted something new—the existence of a DNA genetic code, that is, a "blueprint" for inheritance. The experiments to test for the existence of a DNA genetic code ultimately gave scientists the ability to "read" this code (see

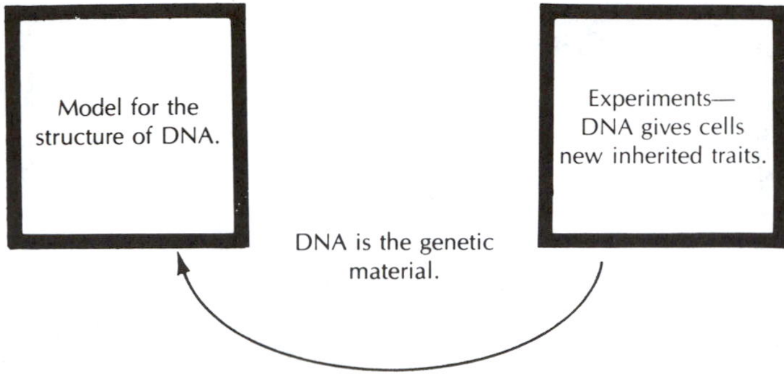

Figure 12.8

Fig. 12.9). Today, not only can we read the genetic code, we can rewrite it as well, a phenomenal achievement of our time.

Other Sciences Supported

We've dealt with physics and chemistry as disciplines supported by strong evidence. Other areas derive great benefit when they can rest on evidence from these disciplines. For example, physics has given astronomers insight into astronomy. They know a great deal about the physical reactions taking place in the sun without ever having been there or experimenting with the sun itself. Physics has also been of help to cosmology (theories of origin and development of the universe); physics and chemistry likewise support geology.

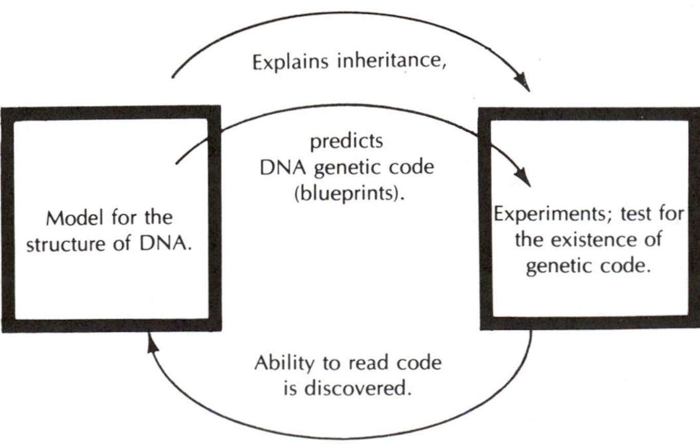

Figure 12.9

Controversial Areas at the Forefront

Although all theories stand ready to be supplanted in the future, some areas are "hot"—most of the research is based there. These controversial areas are rapidly changing as evidence mounts to push the frontier forward. For instance, the cellular theory of sexual reproduction, with its hypotheses of gametes, fertilization, and zygote, was at the forefront of scientific thinking in the nineteenth century but is now not in dispute.[1] Of course, on the cutting edge of scientific thinking, many conflicting theories will remain controversial until exhaustive experimentation points to the more likely theory. For instance, is there an influence of attitude on the causation of disease? Even if a strong correlation were found between those with serious disease and depression, the depression could be the result of being ill, not vice versa. Eventually, better information will strengthen the likelihood of this theory, or it will fail for want of evidence.

CORRELATION

Case Study—A Correlational Tool

As discussed in chapter 4, oftentimes for moral and practical reasons, social, behavioral, and medical scientists cannot run experiments on humans. Researchers have to rely on evidence gained after the fact. We can look through records to find a situation where all variables were held constant except the one we're interested in. The validity of the results will depend on two factors. First, any variables besides the one in question must have in fact stayed constant. Second, many instances of this situation must be found, which often requires sifting through an enormous number of records. Researchers who use this kind of evidence look for correlations between variables.

Correlation and Causation Compared

What is the difference between correlation and causation? With a correlation one can see that there is a relationship between two variables. The relationship can be of two types: It can be a direct (causal) relationship, such that changes in X will bring changes in Y, or it can be the case that X and Y change in response to a third variable, say, W. There is not a direct relationship between X and Y in this second case. That is, if we change X, we will not necessarily see changes in Y (fig. 12.10).

The difficulty of after-the-fact, or case, studies is that although one finds a correlation between variables, this does not mean that a causal relationship has been found. It is much more difficult to be sure that only the variable X in which you are interested is changing while all other

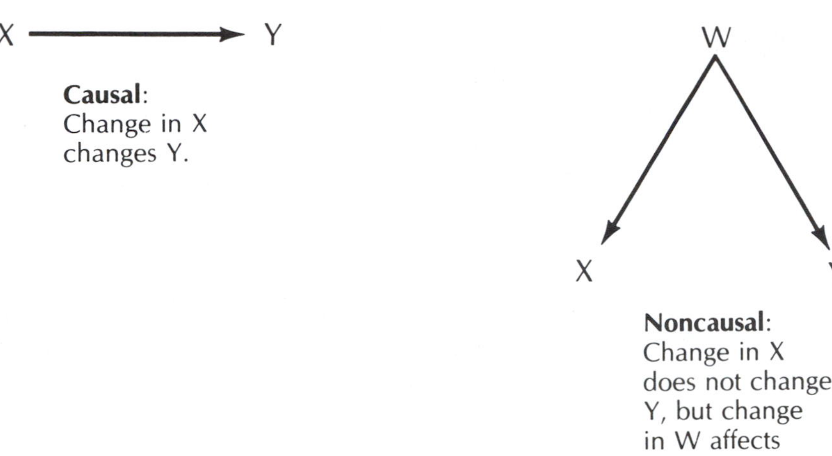

Figure 12.10

important variables, including W, have been held constant. Experiments, however, allow you to manipulate the environment precisely so that you can exclude the possibility that X and Y are moving in response to a third variable.

For example, say that one discovers a correlation between the automobile accidents people are involved in and their proximity to home. Is being close to home causing people to have accidents? The problem is that other variables may be at work. For instance, once it is realized that out of all the miles driven, more would be near home (especially if a person makes many short trips), the causal explanation no longer seems plausible.

Here are three more examples which illustrate the quandary we sometimes face in trying to decide whether a relationship is just a correlation or actually causation.

You recall the brief discussion about smoking and lung cancer in chapter 4. When the correlation was originally found, two possibilities could have explained it. First, smoking could actually cause lung cancer; second, people who had a susceptibility to lung cancer (for some unknown reasons) could also be the same group of people who were heavy smokers (Fig. 12.11). One might fish around for any number of possibilities to explain this correlation. For instance, it is *possible* that people who smoke a lot also drink a lot, and drinking might be the cause of lung cancer. Or perhaps nervousness causes lung cancer, and people who are nervous smoke.

Additional correlation studies between these factors and lung cancer could be made. But far more powerful evidence is an understanding of a

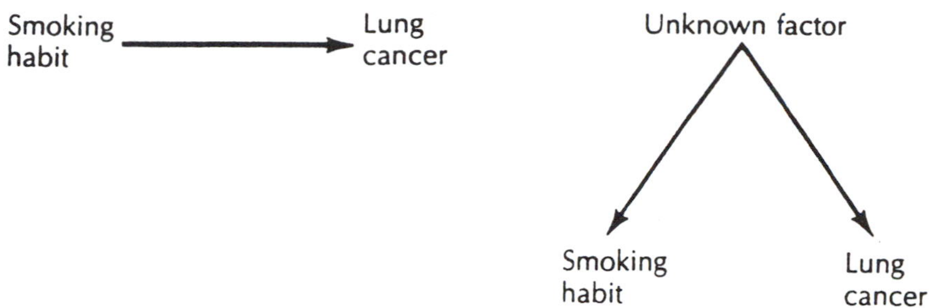

Figure 12.11

direct mechanism whereby cigarette smoking could be causing cancer. Laboratory experiments with the substances found in cigarette smoke have shown these substances to change normal animal cells into cancer cells. Furthermore, experimental evidence strongly suggests that a chemical change in the DNA causes this malignant transformation. In sum, a strong correlation is vastly reinforced by direct experimental evidence.

There is some correlation between milk consumption and the incidence of cancer in various societies. The milk *might* be causing the cancer, but this correlation is probably explained by the relative wealth of these societies, which allows more people to buy milk as well as to live longer (the longer one lives the greater the chance that one's body will on its own make the "mistakes" in cell division that lead to cancer).

As a third example, there is a well-known positive correlation between the number of Baptist ministers and the per capita liquor consumption in cities with populations over 10,000 in the United states. We can either blame the Baptist ministers for this lamentable condition, or search for some other more likely cause of these two phenomena occurring at the same time (fig. 12.12). The most likely explanation is probably trivial: More Baptist (and other) ministers and higher per capita liquor consumption occur in larger cities. However, there is not necessarily any causal relation between liquor consumption and number of Baptist ministers.

In short, strong correlations are important in pointing out possible causal relationships but in themselves aren't definitive evidence of a causal relationship.

The Significance of Increasing Knowledge

We tend to forget the amount of knowledge we have accumulated over the centuries and how our everyday lives have been affected. The following reconstruction of the mental outlook in Europe six hundred years ago should be enlightening.

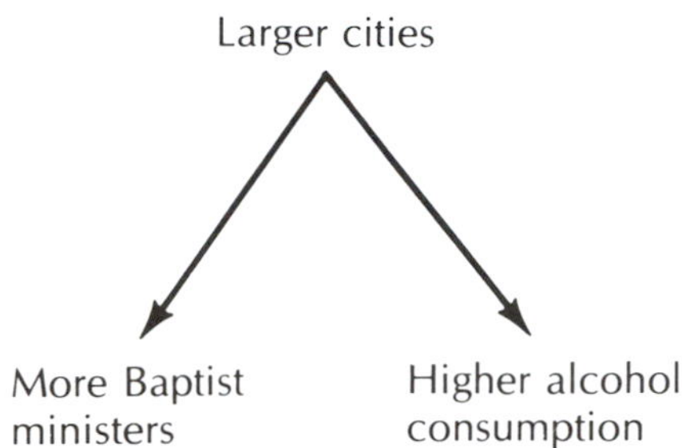

Figure 12.12

Imagine that you live in fourteenth-century Europe. Suddenly, half your family and neighbors develop strange black swellings about the size of an apple or egg in the armpits and groin. These swellings ooze blood and pus and are followed by spreading boils and black blotches on the skin from internal bleeding. Many in your town are suffering severe pain and dying quickly after five days, or sometimes overnight. The disease spreads. Then other symptoms, continuous fever and the spitting of blood, appear instead of the swellings. Everything that issues from the sick—breath, sweat, blood from the swellings, bloody urine, and blood-blackened excrement—smells foul. You and everyone around you are terrified, desperately seeking an explanation in order to save yourselves from pain, deformity, and death.

Alas, given the lack of knowledge at this time in the areas of physiology, biology, and pharmacology, the explanations available to you will not help. You are used to living among rats and fleas, so nothing in your understanding would lead you to ascribe the cause of the disease to these creatures, since people lived with them before the bubonic plague began. Your most acute observation of rats running down the gangplanks of cargo ships that carry diseased sailors would therefore not enable you to make the mental jump (hypothesis) to rats as disease-carriers, because no understanding of animal and insect-borne contagion exists. To further complicate matters, there is also a pneumonic form of the disease, carried by microorganisms in the air, but of course you don't know about microorganisms.

Here are some of your fourteenth-century contemporaries' attempts to explain the plague:

1. Poisoned air and stinking mists from stagnant lakes are poisoning people.
2. People fall ill by looking at sick people, who "dart death from their eyes."
3. The planets are conjoined in a way that causes the plague.
4. God is visiting His wrath on mankind for its sins.
5. The Jews are poisoning the wells, hoping to murder all Christians.

Here are the accompanying remedies, in the same order:

1. To draw poison from the body, bleed it, purge it with laxatives, or apply hot plasters. In addition, give these medicines: powdered stag's horn, compounds of rare spices, powdered pearls or emeralds mixed into potions. Other recommendations: Eat a bland diet, avoid excitement, go to the public latrine, and smell the foul odors, which are curative (avoid swamps, however, which cause the plague).
2. Avoid anyone suffering from the plague, even your parents or child. Don't visit the sick or bury the dead.
3. Wait for the planets to change their positions.
4. Join a penitents' procession, lasting up to three days and attended by as many as two thousand people, to pray for God's mercy. Stop doing anything that could anger Him, including gambling, cursing, and drinking. Or join the flagellates, whose members go from town to town whipping themselves for mankind's sins and exhorting others to atone.
5. Attack the Jews.

Unhappily, all of these expedients were attempted. The second, cruel as it was, probably worked best. Many realized that the charge against the Jews was ridiculous (Jews were dying at the same rate as Christians), but even the pleadings of the Pope could not stop mobs in many cities from burning thousands of people to death.

The medical faculty of the University of Paris, and doubtless many others, realized that the cause of the plague was not known. It would be five hundred years before its cause, the microscopic bacillus *Pasteurella pestis*, was discovered. It lives alternately in the stomach of the flea and the bloodstream of the rat—the bite of flea or rat transmits the disease. It is now believed that caravans carried rats with the bacillus out of Central Asia, where it was further spread by rats on cargo ships. When the plague raged, India, China, North Africa, and Europe suffered huge casualties, possibly 30 to 50 percent of their populations. Because they were not understood and thereby checked, the plague and other epidemics returned for centuries, racking Europe, Asia, and Africa.[2]

A Modern Contrast

The discovery of a virus involved in Acquired Immune Deficiency Syndrome (AIDS) within three years of its detection makes a startling contrast with the half-millenium required to understand bubonic plague. The contrast is especially impressive, since the mechanism underlying AIDS is more complicated. This initial understanding was not achieved, however, without a monumental collaboration of thousands of scientists and $80 million in research grants to abet scientific understanding of the immune system. Compared to the five hundred years it took to cure bubonic plague, one can only assume that a cure for AIDS is right around the corner, relatively speaking.

VITAL SPECULATION

Thanks to science, we have longer life spans, better health, bigger bridges, and more powerful weapons. But what on earth should we *do* with them?

Science and its consequent technology have increased human capabilities enormously, creating an ever-enlarging blank slate for our pleasure. Decisions about whether and how to use our new techniques are value judgments that we must make. Value judgments which arise out of controversial, subtle arguments in the social sciences and humanities enable us to "write" on that ever-expanding blank slate of human capabilities. In the social sciences, for example, historical arguments can suggest national policy; evidence from anthropology and sociology help us rethink our cultural assumptions. Besides sheer enjoyment in studying them, the humanities afford us a range of life options that we could never have invented as individuals. World literature is a window into possible or actual states of awareness and ways of life. And philosophers thrive on arguments, speculating about the basic assumptions of other disciplines and even the nature of philosophy itself.

All of the readings in this book are speculative arguments. Four will appear at the end of this chapter. Two are about the nature of literature, one about science, and the last about the nature of the major subject areas.

EVALUATING

The foregoing chapter was a second sketch, an overlay to chapter 4. The significant point is that as you evaluate an argument, keep the general subject area in mind. Is this an argument about the material world? Then wherever possible its evidence should be founded on the scientific method. Is it an argument about the "social world"? Then usually expect correlative studies and evaluate their adequacy. Is it a prescriptive or values argument? Look for a general principle and persuasive examples from common experience.

Remember that no matter what sort of evidence is presented, you're not forced to accept or reject an argument totally, but have a range of options. (Review "Good Arguments Should Admit Their Limits," in chapter 4.) An argument might present little evidence, some evidence, good, or even very strong evidence, compared to alternative arguments or hypotheses.

Outside the Pale

What about a study such as astrology? Is it mere academic prejudice that this subject is not included as a serious pursuit? After all, many people have been surprised to learn that their behavior matches what their sign predicts about them. Isn't this good evidence that astrology is onto the truth about human nature and should be carefully studied?

It can be argued that astrology is rigid where it should be flexible and flexible where it should be more rigorous. It's a dogma, not a hypothesis, that anyone born between March 21 and April 20 is, as an Aries, going to be more aggressive than a person born under another sign. (One piece of evidence—Hitler was an Aries.) This is a *dogma*, not a hypothesis, because astrologers, unlike scientists, are unwilling to modify their notion of an Aries upon receipt of evidence, say, that many people born during this time are not more aggressive.

An astrologer might counterargue, "Well, that's just the point. Every Aries is in fact more aggressive! You can't find any evidence to the contrary. Show me an Aries and I will show you a more aggressive person." We would cite as counterevidence the poet William Wordsworth, also an Aries (April 7), but not a person known to be aggressive.

In the spirit of balance let's reply, O.K., maybe you're right. But this aggression could still be in the eye of the beholder-astrologer and not in the Aries person. Let's adopt the scientific stance and take the "Aries notion" as a hypothesis to be tested. (Thus we will put the predictive power of astrology to the test.) If those born under the sign of Aries are in fact more aggressive, astrologers should be able to detect that aggression without being told the person's sign. In that spirit of inquiry, how about the following experiment:

A number of people present themselves to an astrologer. The one thing that they may *not* tell the astrologer is their birth dates; however, the astrologer may conduct any sort of personality test, with the subjects doing their best to answer truthfully. Now, can the astrologer successfully *predict* which people are born under the sign of Aries? Even a 50 percent success rate that could be repeated anytime would be impressive. It would be impressive, but only as a beginning. For instance, it has been claimed that people often like best the season in which they were born. If this is true and if the astrologer asks what a person's favorite time of year is, he has improved his chances of guessing a person's sign from one in twelve to one in three. The way around this possible leak would be to prohibit the subjects from telling their favorite season. The question always remains whether there is some other variable at work helping the results along, but that is what the community of thinkers is for.

Even after numerous successes, more carefully controlled (correlative) tests would have to be run to detect what this "aggression" actually is, in order to define it narrowly enough so that one could successfully predict behaviors that an Aries would engage in and those that she would not. Then those predictions would have to be traced, preferably without the subjects' or the "aggression" evaluator's knowing the purpose of the experiment.

Finally, what is the *precise* causal connection between the planets and personality? The dogma of astrology does not (yet?) rest on physics or astronomy, and it doesn't (yet) fit into the body of established knowledge hard-won through scientific method. Current theories of physics would have it that the doctor at the newborn's bedside exerts a gravitational pull many times greater than that of the nearest planet. No relationship between gravitation and personality has been established to date. (See also John Paulos's objections to astrology in chapter 10, page 129).

SUMMARY

The three major types of evidence and their characteristics are:

1. *Experimental:* Evidence gathered by cycling from scientific experiment to model change to new experiment.
2. *Correlative:* Evidence gathered by detecting relationships between two variables which may or may not be causally related.
3. *Speculative:* The use of a general principle and persuasive examples from common experience as evidence.

Our increase in knowledge has resulted in startling changes in the way we live and view the world.

To assess evidence (review chapter 4), ask the following questions: What *kind of evidence* does the argument provide—experimental, correlative, or speculative? Given the kind of evidence possible in that subject area, is the evidence in this argument appropriate? If you know of any alternative arguments, do you find the evidence in the argument at hand to be *nonexistent, slight, good, strong, or compelling?*

If you give any evidence more credence than it deserves, little harm is done as long as you maintain the balance discussed throughout this book.

EXERCISES

1. What kind of evidence would you expect in the following arguments: experimental, correlative, or speculative?

   That crime is caused by a bad environment
   That human nature is evil
   That growing cacti can reward you
   That Roosevelt knew that Japan would bomb Pearl Harbor
   That supply-side economics reduces inflation
   That philosophers should deal with the language contained in factual claims, and not with values
   That treating moths with a certain pheromone (insect hormone) will make them sterile
   That the origin of the American slang term "copacetic" probably came from the Yiddish *kol ba seder,* meaning that all goes well.

2. What if the astrologer countered that he couldn't predict who would be an Aries because their entire astrological chart had to be taken into account? The Aries with, say, lots of passive Pisces in her chart would not emerge as an overall Aries. Everyone has a rising sign, a moon sign, and signs in twelve houses, which represent areas of life such as "marriage" and "career," as well as planets distributed in various houses. Can you come up with any ideas to test this more complicated hypothesis?

READINGS

1. In this excerpt from a revealing essay, Czech novelist Milan Kundera argues that the purpose and greatness of the novel lie in its asking questions about human experience that only the novel can ask. Unlike science, however, there are no precise answers, and to interpret one character's experience as closer to the truth than that of another character is to distort the novel's understanding of life's complexity.

The rise of science propelled man into the tunnels of specialized knowledge. With every step forward in scientific knowledge, the less clearly he could see either the world as a whole or his own self. . . .

If one accepts as a hypothesis that philosophy and science have ignored man's being, then it is even clearer that Cervantes gave birth to a great European art which is nothing other than the perpetual investigation of the being ignored by science. . . . The novel discovered the different dimensions of existence one by one: with Cervantes and his contemporaries, it questioned the nature of adventure; with Richardson, it began to examine "what happens inside" and to unmask the secret life of feelings; with Balzac, it discovered man's rootedness in history; with Flaubert, it explored the *terra* previously *incognita* of the everyday; with Tolstoy, it focused on the role of the irrational in human behavior and decisions. It measured time; the evanescent past with Proust, the evanescent present with Joyce. With Thomas Mann, it queried the role of the myths that control our movements from the remote past of man. And so on, and so on.

The novel has accompanied man uninterruptedly and faithfully since the beginning of the Modern Era. It was then that the "passion of knowing," which [the philosopher] Husserl considered to be the essence of European spirituality, seized the novel and led it to observe man's concrete life closely, and to protect him from "the forgetting of [his own] being." . . . The only *raison d'être* [rationale] for a novel is to discover what can only be discovered by a novel. A novel that does not uncover a hitherto unknown segment of existence is immoral. Knowledge is the novel's only morality. . . .

Kundera goes on to define the "knowledge" that the novel gives. Note how it contrasts with scientific knowledge:

To take the world as relative, as Cervantes does, to be obliged to face not a single absolute truth but a heap of contradictory truths (truths embodied in *imaginary thinking selves* called characters), to have as one's only certainty the *wisdom of uncertainty*, requires . . . [heroic] courage.

Who's right and who's wrong? Don Quixote or the [other characters]? Much has been written on the question. Some see in Cervantes's novel a rationalist critique of Don Quixote's wooly idealism. Others see the novel as a celebration of the same idealism. Both interpretations are mistaken because they both try to find at the novel's source not a question but a moral judgment.

Man desires a world where good and evil are clearly distinguished. He has an innate and inextinguishable tendency to make judgments before he understands. Religions and ideologies are founded on this desire. But they can cope with the novel only by translating its language of relativity and ambiguity into their own . . . dogmatic tongue. . . . Either [Kafka's character] K., crushed by an unjust court, is innocent, or the court stands for divine justice and K. is guilty.

This "either-or" encapsulates an inability to bear the essential relativity of human affairs. This inability means that the novel's wisdom (the wisdom of uncertainty) is hard to accept or to grasp.[3]

2. John Gardner's argument about the purpose of literature differs somewhat from Kundera's. In your opinion, are their views compatible?

The writing of fiction is a mode of thought because by imitating we come to understand the thing we imitate. Fiction is thus a convincing and honest but unverifiable science (in the old sense, knowledge): unverifiable because it depends on the reader's sensitivity and clear sense of how things are, a sense for which we have no tests. Some people claim our basic human nature is vicious, some claim otherwise. The cynic can be shown, by definition, to be a cynic, but he cannot be proved wrong. (So far, unhappily, it cannot even be proved conclusively that he grows ulcers more quickly than do nice people.) Therefore, the kind of knowledge that comes from imitation depends for its quality on the sanity and stability of the imitator. Clearly no absolute standard for sanity and stability exists, but rough estimates are possible. If a writer regularly treats all life bitterly, scorning love, scorning loyalty, scorning decency (according to some standard)—or, to put it another way, if some writer's every remark strikes most or many readers as unfair, cruel, stupid, self-regarding, ignorant, or mad; if he has no good to say of anything or anyone except the character who seems to represent himself; if he can find no pleasure in what happy human beings have found good for centuries (children and dogs, God, peace, wealth, comfort, love, hope, and faith)—then it is safe to hazard that he has not made a serious effort to sympathize and understand, that he has not tried to guess what special circumstances would make him behave, himself, as his enemies behave. . . . Whatever some possible divinity might say of such a writer's fictions, the nonomniscient can say this much: he is not using fiction as a mode of thought but merely as a means of preaching his peculiar doctrine. . . .[4]

3. Compare the foregoing arguments about literature with this one about the nature of science:

[Scientific] objectivity is closely bound up with the *social aspect of scientific method,* with the fact that science and scientific objectivity do not (and cannot) result from the attempts of an individual scientist to be "objective," but from the *friendly-hostile co-operation of many scientists. . . .*

Two aspects of the method of the natural sciences are of importance in this connection. Together they constitute what I may term the "public character of scientific method." First, there is something approaching *free criticism.* A scientist may offer his theory with the full conviction that it is unassailable. But this will not impress his fellow-scientists and competitors; rather it challenges them: they know that the scientific attitude means criticizing everything, and they are little deterred even by authorities. Secondly, scientists try to avoid talking at cross-purposes. (I may remind the reader that I am speaking of the natural sciences, but a part of modern economics may be included.) They try very seriously to speak one and the same language, even if they use different mother tongues. In the natural sciences this is achieved by recognizing experience as the impartial arbiter of their controversies. When speaking of "experience" I have in mind experience of "public" character, like observations, and experiments, as opposed to experience in the sense of more "private" aesthetic or religious experience, and an experience is "public" if everybody who takes the trouble can repeat it. In order to avoid speaking at cross-purposes, scientists try to express their theories in such a form that they can be tested, i.e., refuted (or else corroborated) by such experience.

This is what constitutes scientific objectivity. Everyone who has learned the technique of understanding and testing scientific theories can repeat the experiment and judge for himself. . . .[5]

4. This last passage is a rich series of arguments about the nature of various disciplines. It deserves a good deal of thought and affords any number of comparisons with the foregoing three arguments.

Value and meaning traditionally have been the preserve of the humanities, which depict their nature, present instances, describe or inspire their pursuit, and portray their role or their absence in our lives. Philosophy, too, can fall within this domain. Before describing how philosophy can be carried on as part of the humanities, we must pause to describe the intellectual and imaginative landscape.

The sciences aim at truths and explanations; it is the highest ambition of current scientists to discover and formulate new important truths, laws, and explanations that will be incorporated into the textbooks of the future. No physicist, biologist, or economist now expects or even hopes that the articles or books he writes will themselves be read one hundred years from now. These are not designed to be read or experienced directly; the truths they discover and laws they formulate can just as well be present in other people's words—and they will be as they are incorporated into the larger edifice of scientific truths and textbooks. When, occasionally, an elder scientist writes his autobiography or presents general thoughts on the nature of his scientific activity, he is well aware that he is not doing science.

Works of art and literature, on the other hand, are produced with the intention that they will be experienced directly. No one now thinks it is unnecessary to read Shakespeare because everything important in him has been incorporated into current literature. However, although these works of art are produced with the intention that they will be read or experienced directly, it is not intended usually that they present truths or explanations, unless "imaginative" ones—truths of another sort. Since the "truths" they contain are not extractable or paraphrasable without loss, it is not surprising that these works must be experienced directly and so cannot merely be incorporated into future texts or re-presentations. . . .

There is a body of writing, however, which intends both to present truths, explanations, and so on, and to be read directly rather than merely incorporated into other writings. Here fall the great works of political philosophy (of Plato, Aristotle, Hobbes, Locke, Rousseau), of social theory (Marx, Tocqueville, Weber, Durkheim), of moral theory, of religious thought, of philosophy generally. The writers of these works strive after truths, yet view it as important and write with the intention that their works themselves will be read, that their own voice will be heard. With an aim of science (to produce truths and explanation) yet an intention of artistic works (to be experienced directly), these works present a puzzle. Why should it be important that works presenting truths be experienced directly? What accounts for this phenomenon in works of the humanities?

The humanities are marked by (the nature of) their concern with value and meaning. . . . Yet, not every concern with value and meaning falls within the humanities; for example, consider the way an anthropologist can study the values of different cultures or tribes, make cross-cultural comparisons of value, and so forth. The anthropologist studies values by placing them in quotation marks, telling us: "they believe it is wrong to eat meat, marry one's uncle or aunt, allow an insult to go unavenged." The anthropologist's report of these beliefs neither endorses nor condemns them; from the anthropological report no value statement follows. Values can be the subject matter of the anthropologist's study, but as a social scientist his standpoint toward these is external. He could just as well be describing (or trying to explain) different values, or things other than values. He does not respond internally to them; he does not respond to values qua values. The quotation marks are the fence that keeps him external to the values.

[On the other hand,] a work of the humanities responds to value as value, to meaning as meaning, and it is concerned with these in relation to humanity, as they guide or inspire human affairs; so, the humanities are concerned with. . . . the value and meaning we bring into the world and exhibit through our free choices. . . .

The poet, painter, or critic is responding to value as value, meaning as meaning, and he also has an audience in mind; he intends that through the object he makes (poem, painting, essay) or the activity he performs, the audience will also respond to the values and meanings he is responding to. . . . Also, the artist (often? always?) intends that his product have a value of its own that will be responded to by the audience. . . .

The search for explanations itself lifts us out of our narrow concerns; and the free consideration of possibilities, placing a matter within a wider matrix of possibilities, not only increases understanding but enables us to transcend the limits of the actual. . . .

Cannot scientific explanations also be offered in a quest for valuable theoretical unifications in nature, as a vehicle whereby we can respond to that value as the scientist does, and to the value of his so responding? Why cannot science be carried on as part of the humanities? The motivation of scientists often is to discern and uncover the deep unifying principles underlying diverse phenomena, and their motivation even can be to remove unsightly theoretical blemishes, coincidences, tensions, rather than to account directly for observed facts. . . .

To investigate the ways science is or can be humanistic, to discern its humanistic strands, is not to recommend *transforming* it further, against its grain, into a humanity or into something with humanistic veneer. Yet the investigation is worth making, for the sciences are a dominant part of the modern intellectual world, and the scientific picture of the world, the "scientific outlook," appears to leave no room for value and meaning, and so threatens the very legitimacy of the humanities. . . . It is ironic that one of the most glorious achievements of the modern mind, science, seems to leave no room for its own glory; that the reduced image of man toward which it seems inexorably to lead—a mean and pitiable plaything of forces beyond his control—seems to leave no room even for the creators, and the creation, of science itself.[6]

NOTES

[1]Ralph W. Lewis, Letter, *Scientific American*, April 1984, p. 6.

[2]Adapted from Barbara Tuchman, *A Distant Mirror: The Calamitous 14th Century* (New York: Ballantine Books, 1978), pp. 92–126.

[3]Milan Kundera, "The Novel and Europe," *New York Review of Books*, July 19, 1984, p. 15.

[4]John Gardner, *On Moral Fiction* (New York: Basic Books, Inc., 1978), pp. 116–17.

[5]Karl R. Popper, *The Open Society and Its Enemies* (Princeton, N.J.: Princeton University Press, 1971), II, pp. 217–18.

[6]Robert Nozick, *Philosophical Explanations* (Cambridge, Mass.: Harvard University Press, 1981), pp. 619–21, 625–27.

CHAPTER THIRTEEN

FLIMSY STRUCTURES

This chapter could have been titled "*Un*warranted Inferences." The following are certain infamous reasons given to support arguments—infamous because they mimic real support. There are two basic replies to these inferences: "So what?" or "What else?"

Abusing arguments may be among the world's older professions. Proper names for many types of abuse are in Latin. I'll deal only with the seven deadliest: inconsistency, ad hominem attacks, appeal to pity, begging the questions, post hoc ergo propter hoc, appeal (only) to the many, and straw man.

INCONSISTENCY

Two main ways of being inconsistent come to mind:

1. *Offering reasons that are contradictory*

For example, arguing that most people who strive for success do so out of hunger for love and admiration they didn't get when growing up; and in the same book arguing that most people strive for success because they can afford to take the risk of failure, having been given a lot of encouragement and attention as children. Since encouragement and attention are tantamount to love and admiration, this argument is foundering on inconsistency unless the arguer makes a careful distinction between the pairs of terms *love-admiration* and *encouragement-attention* to explain this disparity.

2. *Offering reasons which contradict the conclusion*

For example, We should conserve on fuel because many of the elderly poor are dying from lack of heat in the winter.

Given that reason, the conclusion would appear to be the opposite: that we should expend more fuel, at least on the elderly poor (unless some fiend is advocating killing off the elderly poor).

Enjoy Being on the Lookout

You can enjoy ferreting out inconsistencies (rather like the children's game "What's wrong with this picture?" in which the flag and the wind sock are flying in opposite directions, with the rabbit upside down under the hedge).

Discoveries can be fascinating. For instance, employers frequently advertise themselves as "equal opportunity affirmative action employer." But the only case in which an employer could be both is when the minority or woman applying is more qualified than any white male applicant. In cases of a "tie," or when a white male is better qualified, something has to give. Think about whether these two often-connected terms, "equal opportunity" and "affirmative action," can be reconciled.

Reconciling Differences

Anyone who is at cross-purposes with his own ideas has just shot himself in the foot, argumentatively speaking. The hearer's appropriate response to inconsistent arguments is "So what?"

One can let the argument drown in its own juices. But, depending on how interested one is in the subject, a lot of fun can be had trying to reconcile these differences ("What else would reconcile these inconsistencies? Is that something else true?").

Carefully check your work to make sure you're not involved in major inconsistencies. Students sometimes say, "I know my major reasons look inconsistent on paper. But I had such-and-such other idea in mind when I wrote this, so the reasons really do fit." For heaven's sake! Don't expect your reader to be a mind reader as well. It's only fun to ferret out inconsistencies when they're subtle. Those that glare are painful.*

*For a discussion of consistency, its relationship to warranted inference, and language with which to point to inconsistencies, review chapter 5.)

AD HOMINEM ATTACK

Ad hominem argument is the formal name for name-calling. *Ad hominem* literally means "against the man."

> The author was **guilty of an ad hominem argument** when he impugned Ms. Manners's reputation instead of discussing her ideas.
>
> It's a shame that the discussion **sank to the level of ad hominem argumentation.** Dislike of a person's affiliations **is not relevant** to the issue.

Ad hominem attack is the discounting of another person's ideas by *discounting the person* instead of showing why the idea is not good. The name-caller is off the issue.

Varieties of this logical sin can be blatant. For example: "Don't listen to Betty; she's a real dope." The answer should be something like "So what if you think she's a dope? What is her argument?" Other times ad hominem attack can be subtle: "Politicians are busy at this time advocating reduced taxes as a way to improve their image with the public." So what is their argument to reduce taxes?

The salient points should have been *what* Betty's and the politicians' arguments are and *why* these arguments should be discounted or accepted. So what if the counterarguer thinks that Betty is a dope and politicians are image-polishers?

The assumptions beneath the conclusion that name-calling is a pitfall are, as always, that everyone is a member of the community of thinkers and no one should be excluded. Of course, the people we want to exclude are the people whom we dislike. With so many juicy things we can say against our neighbor, it's often easier to backbite than to bother with the argument at hand.

In defense of name-calling, one might argue that life is short, the tasks are many, and name-calling is a kind of a shorthand ("consider the source") which helps us make quick decisions and eliminate silly notions. Even granting that, every time we use this shorthand we've robbed ourselves of the reward of some intellectual discovery, perhaps why a Communist's advocacy of state ownership of the means of production is not a good idea. Although dealing with the unpleasant ideas of unpleasant people involves facing the fear that they may end up convincing us that they're right, we can only act as fair-minded critical thinkers in the hope that they (who doubtless also find us unpleasant) will be similarly moved by *our* alternative arguments and that the best approximation of the truth will out.

APPEAL TO PITY

It is all right to appeal to pity when it is directly related to the issue. Here is an example: "The Lilliputians are in great pain and starving. Please take pity on them and give money to the Fund for the Lilliputian people." Of course, before we dig into our pockets, we might want to check whether the Lilliputians are in fact starving and whether the fund is reputable. Still, the argument that we should help fellow human beings out of pity because they are in pain offers a *relevant* reason, even if it turns out that the whole thing is bogus—Lilliputians, fund, and all.

What is neither ethical nor logical is switching tracks, evoking sympathies for one issue and transferring them to another.* Say, for example, that a professor tells her students to write especially favorable evaluations of her because she's coming up for tenure and really needs the job. While it may be a piteous thing indeed for all concerned if she is fired, the only *relevant* reasons for good evaluations must lie in the professor's performance as a teacher.

These are, it is hoped, clear-cut cases. There are others in which the distinction between legitimate and illegitimate appeal to pity is blurred. Let's consider the current debate on affirmative action ("affirmative action" here defined as the deliberate hiring of qualified women and minorities, these women and minorities not necessarily being the best qualified among all applicants). The first argument is one in favor.

> Since many white males unavoidably perceive women and minorities as less capable than themselves, there must be affirmative action in hiring. As things stand, most white males enjoy positions of greater money and power than most minorities and women. These historically disadvantaged groups will continue to suffer from job discrimination unless a mandatory affirmative action policy is instituted in all businesses. Out of compassion and fellow feeling (on which, after all, justice is founded), we should have affirmative action.

The next argument is one against affirmative action.

> Most people, white males included, now perceive women and minorities as having capabilities equal to those of white males. Granting that white males enjoy many more positions of money and power, the reason is that minorities and women have not until recently striven for these positions. Hard work and demonstrated abil-

*The Latin name, *argumentum ad misericordiam*, is rarely used.

ity should be the determinants in all hiring decisions, not sympathy for past disadvantages. After all, strict equality of opportunity (on which true justice is founded) is color and sex *blind;* affirmative action is highly color- and sex-conscious, to the deliberate disadvantage of one group.

What is a compassionate and fair-minded person to do?

In such cases, proceed to the question "What else?" Here there is a basic conflict over whether white males perceive women and minorities as equally capable. And it is on this disagreement that the further disagreement whether an appeal to pity is relevant rests. So what else in the form of *evidence* is there that might resolve this conflict? Public opinion polls or sociological studies of attitudes towards women and minorities? What else is there in the way of values *assumptions* beneath each of these arguments? And what are the *implications* of both positions? These arguments were quite brief. What additional *reasons* might support each position?

In sum, when you feel the tug of an emotional appeal, ask *whether the emotion is relevant (so what?).* If you can't decide whether the pity is relevant, look at other aspects of the argument and its counterargument (*what else?*).

Language with which to complain about irrelevant pity is:

The professor's **appeal to pity was irrelevant to the question whether** her performance as an instructor was good.

BEGGING THE QUESTION

You've already encountered this fallacy in chapter 5. It is asserting reasons which are the same as the conclusion. Remember Woody Allen's "Money is better than poverty, if only for financial reasons" or President Calvin Coolidge's remark, "When large numbers of people are out of work, unemployment results." It's fairly easy to spot the fallacy in these one-liners; it's harder to detect in longer arguments, where the conclusion may be separated from the reasons by a number of other claims. A bit of thought comparing the conclusion and reason will reveal this pitfall, however. The conclusion should not be the reason dressed in another form. Here are a few illustrations of how to point out this fallacy:

When the author argued that we should no longer have grades because standards of evaluation ought not to exist, **he begged the question why** we should no longer have grades.

To argue that we are happy because we are content **is to beg the question why** we are happy.

An answer that is completely off the subject is also called begging the question:

> When they asked him why he committed the murder, he asked them what right they had to know, **thus begging the question of** his motives.

In the case of arguments for which evidence can be obtained, we should take a dim view of people wasting our time with question-begging arguments. One exception which might earn our indulgence, though not necessarily our acceptance of their conclusions, is the case of arguments about God.

Strong evidence demonstrating anything about God is notoriously scarce. Yet in his excellent text on fallacies, author S. Morris Engel asserts that the following is fallacious because circular:

> The world is good because God is good. God is good because the world is good.[1]

Since we have no way to get universally agreed-upon evidence, this argument should not be considered fallacious, since it is a good try under the circumstances. And certainly the arguer didn't beg the question entirely, claiming that the world is good because the world is beneficent, or that God is good because God is kind. Or do you agree with Engel? The word "good" certainly begs for definition.

Or consider this case: Painter Salvador Dali is said to have remarked that DNA proves that God exists. Extrapolating from that statement, consider:

> If DNA exists, God exists. If God exists, some organizing principles of nature such as DNA exist.

POST HOC ERGO PROPTER HOC: ARGUING THAT WHAT FOLLOWS A THING MUST BE CAUSED BY IT

Do you see why the Latin, although long, is better than the longer English? The Latin is, literally, "after this, therefore because of this."

Post hoc ergo propter hoc is an easy trap to fall into, because our experience is often just that: We observe one thing (a car hitting a post) and figure that what follows has been caused by it (dented fender by post). However, humanity has learned by bitter experience to be cautious in concluding that whatever follows after something *must* be caused by it. Someone, for example, noticed that during the past fifty years whenever women's hemlines have risen, the economy has improved. Although it is *possible* that an upturn in women's hemlines causes an upturn in the economy, it is too precarious to come to that conclusion *only* because the one event has followed the other. Again, the operative question is "*What else* could be at work here besides causation?" One answer is correlation, with an unknown third factor causing both upturns (see chapters 4 and 12). Another answer is "nothing": It may be a coincidence. (For an excellent discussion of how often people mistakenly draw causal inferences from random events, see John Allen Paulos's book: *Innumeracy: Mathematical Illiteracy and Its Consequences.*[2])

> In concluding that Hal left the party because he was pushed into the pool, Sam **is guilty of the fallacy, post hoc ergo propter hoc.** Indeed, Hal was upset, but the reason he left was to catch a train.

> The stockbrokers thought that the caviar they served their clients clinched the sale. **This is a case of post hoc ergo propter hoc.** The buyers enjoyed the caviar, but they told us that they bought from the stockbrokers because they wanted to reinvest their money quickly.

APPEAL (ONLY) TO THE MANY

If you argue that I should believe something because many people believe it, you've got my attention. But that reason shouldn't on its own convince me or anyone of your argument, since in the past vast numbers of people have believed in one idea, vast numbers of people in the opposite idea. Therefore the sheer popularity of an idea does not guarantee its rightness. The important question to ask is for what reasons (*what else?*) these vast hordes have been thus persuaded.

> Arguing that we should buy seamless silk jeans **just because millions have done so is to commit the fallacy of appeal to the many.** A decision to buy seamless silk jeans should not be based on that sole reason.

If an advertiser is smart, she will go on to give the reasons why so many people have bought her product, telling us how warm and durable silk is and (if it's true) that we need not suffer the expense of dry-cleaning it.

A number of situations on the surface seem to appeal only to the many, but in fact don't. Consider *Consumer Reports* magazine. It is a handy guide if you're thinking of buying some product. You just look up the issue that deals with what you want, say a car, and learn what many owners think about their cars. This might seem like mere appeal to the many. But the distinction here is that the articles always explain *why* owners of various types of products are satisfied, e.g., that they found few defects, or didn't have to make any special repairs. An argument such as "Pontiacs are good cars because many thousands of users have found them to have few defects" is persuasive of that point and not fallacious. However, a decision to buy the car would depend on additional factors of price, gas mileage, and appearance.

On the assumption that people are more rational than not, it is interesting to learn why many have come to a conclusion. This does not mean that you should come to the same conclusion. Nor should you discount an idea just because few people believe it.

STRAW MAN IS DAMNING WITH FAINT PRAISE

People arguing for a position have been known to cast the opposite position in an unnecessarily feeble light. This portrayal of a counterargument as weaker than it is, is making a straw man argument. People who indulge in this fallacy may be fearful or ignorant of a strong counterargument. Detecting this fallacy depends on having already heard a better counterargument, or knowing information with which to construct one. One man's steel can be the other man's straw. Avoidance of straw man arguments is best achieved by full information and rigorous practice arguing against cherished beliefs (see chapter 3 on alternative arguments and chapter 9 on the dialogue).

> The author **set up a straw man argument by alleging that** the only reason for not smoking is to save money.

> In making a strong counterargument at the end of the animal rights essay, the author hoped to **avoid the straw man fallacy.**

SUMMARY

1. Inconsistency: arguing at cross-purposes with oneself
2. Ad hominem attack: attacking the person, instead of examining the idea
3. Appeal to pity: calling on sympathies not directly related to the issue
4. Begging the question: making the reason the same as the conclusion; or totally sidestepping the issue
5. Post hoc ergo propter hoc: automatically concluding that what follows a phenomenon must have been caused by that phenomenon
6. Appeal (only) to the many: arguing that some idea is good only because many people think so
7. Straw man argument: damning the counterargument with scant support

EXERCISES

1. Questions
   a. What connection do fallacies have with the ideas presented in the first chapter?

b. The press frequently offers "image" as the reason a politician advocates some program. Make a noise like a member of the press and counterargue that the press is not guilty of ad hominem argumentation in most of these cases.

2. Spot that fallacy (if you think there is one) in the following:
   a. Someone argues that an idea should be rejected because its proponent is a longtime Democrat.
   b. Someone argues that you should vote Socialist in the next election because the Socialists have taken quite a beating at the polls in the past.
   c. Student to teacher: "Look, you have to give me an A in this class because I need it to graduate."
   d. A close friend rings up and asks you to come right over because he is feeling very lonely and upset.
   e. Sam and Harry are on a hiring committee. Harry argues that the candidate named George would not make a good personnel manager because he was arrogant and hostile during his employment interview.
   f. One scientist says of another, "Don't trust the data about nerve cells that Ted told you he's just gathered. It is faked. Did you know that he had a psychotic break two years ago and has been in a mental institution ever since?"
   g. A great many people are buying a product. They must just be following the herd.
   h. A movie star advertises a brand of cologne.
   i. Parents abuse their children because they are acting out urges to do violence to their offspring.
   j. An actor who has played a doctor on a popular TV series for many years is now advertising medicine for lumbago.
   k. In eighteen out of the past nineteen Superbowl football games, whenever the NFL team has won, the stock market has gone up dramatically the next day. So an NFL win makes the stock market go up.

   Answers: (a) Ad hominem attack. *You* may not see the proponent's being a Democrat as a blot on a person's character—after all, there are many Democrats—but the arguer here seems to think so. In any event, the argument is irrelevant: off the issue of the Democrat's argument. (b) False appeal to pity. (c) False appeal to pity. (d) O.K. (e) O.K. The issue is whether George would make a good personnel manager. Arrogance and hostility in George bear directly on the question. (f) This remark is O.K.; the issue here is the validity of the scientific data, and if it wasn't arrived at by scientific method, that fact is relevant. If the claim about Ted is deliberately untrue, however, call it ad hominem. (g) None of the seven fallacies here, but an unwarranted inference (falsely impugning the many for being mindless). (h) O.K., as long as the actress is seen as an attention-getter and not an authority. (i) Begging the question. (j) False appeal to authority, or close to it. (k) Post hoc ergo propter hoc, unless there is some other digging: How often does the stock market go up dramatically? How about a poll of a representative sample of stock purchasers "the day after," asking what is motivating them to buy?

3. Speculate on this exceptional case.
   a. Because the stakes are so high in criminal proceedings, it is kosher to consider the character of a witness as *major* support in another issue (the guilt or innocence of the defendant). Do you think that this is a good exception to the rule against ad hominem argument? Why or why not?

NOTES

[1]S. Morris Engel, *With Good Reason: An Introduction to Informal Fallacies,* second ed. (New York: St. Martin's Press, 1982), p. 163.

[2]John Allen Paulos, *Innumeracy: Mathematical Illiteracy and Its Consequences* (New York: Hill and Wang, a division of Farrar, Straus and Giroux, 1988).

CHAPTER FOURTEEN

PROBLEM-SOLVING BY WAY OF REVIEW

Since critical thinking is the consideration of alternative arguments in light of their evidence, problem-solving is the consideration of alternative *solutions* in light of their evidence. The solution is equivalent to the conclusion. This is lucky, because it enables us to enlarge the practicality of the book while reviewing its twelve basic features.

WHATEVER THE PROBLEM IS, THAT'S THE ISSUE

Say you're low on money, but you don't know whether to add more hours to your twelve-hours-per-week part-time job while going to school, fearing that working more might jeopardize your education. The initial problem-issue is, therefore, "Should I add more hours to my part-time job?" You have the **alternatives** yes and no to work out first. Write down the possible solutions, followed by the reasons for and against each.

Solution 1: Yes, add hours to my job

POSITIVE REASONS: It would *please my boss,* who might give me a *better recommendation;* it would make me feel more *independent;* I could maintain *contact* with more people by working more.

REASON(S) NOT WORKING MORE IS BAD: Being low on money is *irritating* and demoralizing.

Solution 2: No, don't add hours to my job

POSITIVE REASONS: I'd keep my *time to study;* I'd keep my *time to enjoy* myself; *education* is *more important* than money.

REASON(S) NOT WORKING MORE IS GOOD: If I worked longer, I might become *overtired and drop out* of school.

Order the Reasons

Pick the most urgent reason on each side and label it 1. A bit of thinking will show some reasons to be less significant. For example, more contact with people could be achieved by other activities less time-consuming than additional work, such as study groups or church groups. In fact, more work might not bring you into contact with more people than it does now. Moreover, getting a recommendation from the boss is presumably not nearly as important as finishing your education. And are you thinking important thoughts, studying, and enjoying yourself in the free time you have, or are you more often just passing time?

It is the "reasons not" on both sides that are the primary considerations in this case. What does it matter if education is more important than money if you get irritated by being low on money and drop out, anyway? Yet the foremost worry on the other side creates a bind, because you might drop out of school from overwork. You are caught on the horns of a dilemma. But now you have a clearer idea of what your dilemma is, so you can work on it. The next stage is to define the dilemma.

Definitions

How low on money am I, exactly?

So low that I can't pay for my necessities?

How irritating and demoralizing is it? Irritating enough that I am distracted and thinking about it all the time, or just once or twice a day?

Say that I can pay for the basics but am broke at the end of each month. And say that I am not thinking about it all the time but lately have noticed that I am worrying about it more often (five or six times a day).

Evidence Can Help Break Gridlocks

Sometimes finding out how most people fare in a similar situation can cast a surprising light. Consider this claim by Professor Alexander Astin, from UCLA, based on his educational research:

> One of the most interesting ways to keep students in college now is through jobs. Students who have part-time jobs while enrolled in college have a better chance of finishing than comparable students who have no jobs. This effect is particularly strong if the student lives on campus. Here we have a case where the facts clearly contradict the folklore: Having to work while attending college does not hamper the student's academic progress but rather enhances it. We should add a note of caution here, however. The beneficial effects of work diminish as the number of hours of work exceeds twenty, and if the student has a full-time job the effect is actually reversed: Students who have to work full-time have a decreased chance of finishing college in contrast to students who have no jobs. In short, it would appear that jobs represent a highly effective way of combatting attrition, *provided* that the number of hours worked is limited to twenty per week.
>
> Students who work up to twenty hours per week tend to get better grades than students who don't work.[1]

Amazing—perhaps in setting up the problem as more work versus a better education, I have created a **false dichotomy.** It looks as though people are managing both. But a bit of caution is in order when considering the **nature of the evidence.** The authority is impeccable, but he had to make a correlational study. Persevering students and part-time jobs are strongly correlated, but ask yourself whether some other factor could be causing both of these results, for instance, love of work. Furthermore, might these working students be the kind of people who, even if they didn't work, would stay in school and get *better grades* to boot?

Consider this counterargument. On the other hand, what would be lost by trying it for a while? You could always bail out of the additional work if it got to be too much. So:

Solution 3: On the premise that up to twenty hours of work doesn't seem to hurt the average student, one prescription would be to go ahead and add hours up to a total of twenty, if possible getting my boss to agree to let me go back to twelve hours if twenty prove too arduous.

Alternatives

So far there are three possible solution-conclusions. But we're just warming up. Brainstorming for a while might produce even better ideas to generate money. For instance:

1. belt-tightening, budgeting

I am wasting some money now, for example, buying lunch and

snacks instead of making them, and buying goods at full price instead of sale price. I compute that savings in these areas alone could add up to $100 per month.

Solution 4: Make a realistic but lean budget and stay within it.

2. borrowing

Is there some understanding friend or relative who would stand me to a loan, or even better, a "scholarship" were I to attain a certain grade point average?

3. selling something I own

Do I own some things I don't particularly want? (I should seriously consider whether I might want these valuables in the future! I'll hold off on heirlooms.)

4. getting a job with better pay

What else is there that I could do for more money per hour?* Thus I might either work twelve hours and get more money than at present, or work twenty hours and make a bundle.

Solution 5: Check the want ads and all possible sources for jobs, applying for any likely sounding position.

There are many other places along the list where you could have written in a solution, but chose not to, because that solution—selling your motorcycle, for instance—didn't appeal immediately. Yet you now know that you can return to your list later, choose other options, or generate more.

Create the Grand Solution

Make a list of the possible solutions:

Same hours at same job
More hours at same job
Add hours to total twenty
Budget
Check ads and apply for higher-paying jobs

Some of these solutions are mutually exclusive, others compatible.

*Notice the **assumptions** that better jobs do in fact exist, that I am worthy of them and could get one, that some of the ones I could get would be no more tiring than the one I now have.

The first two are impossible to act on at the same time, but budgeting can occur with any of the others. It's such a good idea that you might pick it for sure. (At this point a good critical question is "Would budgeting be enough?" For the sake of elaborating on the example, say no.) You can also check the want ads, and since no harm and a lot of good can come of it, you could pick that solution too.

Now. If there are some possible jobs, you'll need to pursue them. Proceeding from the premise that you're already in school and working twelve hours per week, keeping the fewer hours for the time being will enable you to hunt for a better job. For the moment, therefore, you've eliminated the option of working longer at your present job. And **accepting** Astin's **inference** that working up to twenty hours per week is normally not academically harmful, you will look for jobs with a wider range of hours without worry that it will damage your education.

If you get a better offer you can take it outright; or if you would rather work for your present boss you can use your better offer as a bargaining chip to see if she might raise your hourly salary to match what you've been offered.

If, after four weeks (longer?), you can't get a different job, you can try the longer hours at the same job. If the longer hours turn out to be burdensome, you can go back to twelve per week, perhaps job-hunting again. If that doesn't turn anything up, you can go back to your problem-solving list to seek other solutions.

As this problem turned out, here are all the presently conceived solutions for use in case of need:

> *budget plus twelve hours at present job plus job hunt for one month* to result in:
> *new higher-paying job or old job with higher pay.* If not, then:
> *old job with more hours plus budget.* If unsatisfactory after one month,
> *old job with twelve hours plus job hunt plus budget.*

You'll see that with other problems, some solutions that make it to the grand finals are then eliminated.

There is nothing more comforting than contingency planning.

If That Decision Was Wrong

Most important decisions are fraught with uncertainty. The **inference** that longer work hours don't hurt an education may be **unwarranted.** But on the **assumption** that money worries will continue, it is reasonable to try working more, based on Astin's **evidence.** The **implications** are uncertain too, but ideally they would include being happier, easier to live with, and more productive. On the other hand, maybe this is not the best solution, after all. The point is to keep an open mind, considering other options and possibilities as they occur.

Working systematically on solutions to major life problems requires a lot of thought and nerve. To fully explore a problem, write, revise, and think at some length. Doing so turns anxiety into an interesting challenge. Further, as with the dialogue and any creative thought, you shouldn't know where your ideas will take you; otherwise, there is no problem.

I hope to have kept faith with the promise in the preface that everything in the book would be practical and that you are more skillfully negotiating your way through the twists and turns of argumentation. More, I hope that you are very curious to know what is engaging the community of thinkers and that you revel in finding out.

NOTE

[1]Alexander W. Astin, "Strengthening Transfer Programs," in *Issues for Community College Leaders in a New Era,* George B. Vaughan and Associates, eds. (San Francisco: Jossey-Bass Publishers, 1983), p. 125.

GLOSSARY

The following is a list of frequently used phrases in argumentation, with some illustrative examples of their use.

Agree to disagree An accord that arguers are at an impasse and shouldn't keep arguing, probably because they will argue in a circle. Arguers should agree to disagree when (1) they need to get more factual evidence, if the argument hinged on a fact, or (2) they need to come up with different approaches or expanded arguments.

Assumption The reason beneath the stated reason(s). Either the author will not state them at all, or the author will announce them by saying, "I am assuming that," or "The assumption here is."

Based on the premise that "Based on the reason (or assumption) that."

Based on the presupposition that Same as "based on the premise that," above.

Because Indicates that a conclusion has preceded and a reason will follow.

Cause See chapter 12.

Critical thinking The consideration of alternative arguments in light of their evidence. (Other writers on critical thinking have slightly different definitions. Robert Ennis defines critical thinking as "reasonably deciding to believe or do something;" Richard Paul argues that it is "dialogical reasoning." Harvey Siegel defines it as "being appropriately moved by reasons.")

Claim Any statement. Claims are provisional, subject to change with new information.

Deduce To arrive at a particular instance that is entailed in a generalization. Often found in the form, "from which we may deduce that." "All our parachutes open when the rip cord is pulled, from which you may deduce that the one you buy from us will open too."

Definition All that is meant to be included in a term.

Distinction (Between two terms) An important difference between two terms.

Draw the inference that Come to the concluson that.

Draw the conclusion that Same as "draw the inference that."

Even granting that . . . still In a counterargument, a technique for accepting or granting the truth of the other person's reason(s), and yet showing how they are consistent with your argument. "Even granting that it is frightening to speak out in a group and that people may think you're stupid, still it is better to speak your mind because the world needs your ideas just as much as it needs anybody else's."

False dichotomy between In a counterargument, the claim that a false distinction has been made. He: "In college, you can either have a lot of fun or you can do a lot of studying." She: "You have created a false dichotomy between having fun and studying. By George, you can have a lot of fun studying!"

Hinges on Usually the argument hinges on, or is dependent on, some outside fact or other argument (e.g., "The argument that most societies have suppressed women hinges on the claim that there is no biological explanation for women's failure to hold positions of power").

If . . . then What follows "if" is the reason; what follows "then" is the conclusion to that statement.

Implications Consequences beyond the conclusion. Either the author does not state them or the author says, "The implications are."

Imply Most frequently found in a counterargument or used by a respondent in a deliberation. It is a request to clarify someone else's conclusion. "You seem to be suggesting a connection between the cultural values held by a group and their average income. Are you implying that most wealth and poverty are the result of these values?" Or you can use it to say what you don't mean: "But I don't mean to imply that." A less frequent but handy use: One idea necessarily involves another (e.g., "Drama implies conflict").

Inductive leap The jump to a general conclusion from a set of particulars. Leaps are necessary, but some leaps are safer than others. Usually used to describe an unsafe one: "In suggesting that . . . on the basis of just a few cases, the author has made too great an inductive leap."

Infer Come to the conclusion that. "From the look of his sweaty body one can infer that he has been doing strenuous exercise," or "We can make the inference that."

Inference The conclusion. "Although he thinks it's right to conclude that we should be patriotic, he doesn't think it right to base this inference on the premise that we are superior to people of other nations."

Issue The topic or subject at hand.

Make the argument Same as "one could argue that." "One could make the argument that."

Necessary cause A factor without which some effect would not occur. "Oxygen is a necessary cause of fire" (no oxygen, no fire). It often takes several necessary causes to create an effect (e.g., to get a rocket into space, or to get to work on time). *See also* Sufficient cause.

Necessarily Must be the case (e.g., "necessarily involves").

Not necessarily Doesn't have to be the case. "Because some people are better at argumentation doesn't necessarily imply (indicate) that they are smarter.

These better arguers have probably just been practicing longer"; often found in the phrases, "does not necessarily imply," "is not necessarily the case."

Ought Usually signals the solution a thinker has arrived at as a result of his conclusion. "Because of the rapid rate at which we're polluting this lake, I conclude that we will not be able to swim in it by 1996. So we ought to find a new lake to pollute (just kidding)." *See also* Should.

Play the devil's advocate Take the opposite point of view. Student to instructor: "I'd like to play the devil's advocate to your position that our class should have an in-class final. Think of all the extra love and attention we could give to your questions if we had lots of time to mull over them at home."

Premise Reason. *See also* Based on the premise that.

That presupposes That requires the assumption (underlying reason) that. "That argument presupposes that everyone is born with equal enthusiasm and talent."

Reason The support for the conclusion; the why. Write, "The reason is," don't write, "The reason is because," because that's redundant. "The reason for her tardiness is her laziness," or "The reason that she is often tardy *is that* the bus schedule is erratic."

Should Signals a solution or a prescription (as opposed to a statement about what the case *is*). See also Ought.

Sufficient cause A cause that by itself will create an effect. "Oxygen is a necessary cause of a fire, but it isn't sufficient. On the other hand, lack of oxygen is a sufficient cause of choking to death."

Therefore Signals that a conclusion must follow and that a reason came before (usually right before, but not always). "She's always up at 4 A.M. Therefore, she's dead tired by 10 P.M."

Warranted inference A phrase to the effect that a conclusion and/or the step from the reason(s) to the conclusion is justified. "Many studies have found a positive correlation between the amount of time students spend on a course and their grades. These studies warrant the inference that sheer effort expended is a central factor in doing well in school."

INDEX